FIRMLY PLANTED

AND

GROWING

Amy J. Stimson

FIRMLY
PLANTED
AND
GROWING

A Guide for New Christians

AMY L. STRAUSSER

A Division of WINEPRESS PUBLISHING

Unless otherwise noted, all Scriptures are taken from the Holy Bible, New International Version, Copyright © 1973, 1978, 1984 by the International Bible Society. Used by permission of Zondervan Publishing House. The "NIV" and "New International Version" trademarks are registered in the United States Patent and Trademark Office by International Bible Society.

Scripture references marked KJV are taken from the King James Version of the Bible.

Scripture references marked NASB are taken from the New American Standard Bible, © 1960, 1963, 1968, 1971, 1972, 1973, 1975, 1977 by The Lockman Foundation. Used by permission.

ISBN 1-4141-0122-8
Library of Congress Catalog Card Number: 2004100815

Dedication

This book is dedicated to Jim, my husband of 33 years, my daughters, Nancy and Margie, and their husbands Ryan and John.

I wish to thank them for their love and support.

Contents

About This Study

Firmly Planted and Growing is a study designed to compare the complete spiritual development of a Christian—from tender beginnings to maturity—with the growth of a single plant. It is a guide to the successful growth and the development of a new Christian and at the same time explores the amazing similarities with a seed, as it is planted and grows to flower and fruit. It is not an attempt to cover every aspect of the Christian life, but lays a solid foundation on which to build. Christians who are in the growing process can find instruction in this study and learn from Scripture what it means to continue to grow and walk with the Lord toward spiritual maturity. Its teachings are taken directly from God's infallible Word, the Bible.

For your convenience all Scripture for this study is included and is taken from the New International Version Bible. As you study God's Word, I suggest you read it aloud. This helps to maintain good concentration and brings to life the written Word. The format is appropriate for individual or group study. Questions are answered in the back of the book.

All instructional information about plant growth is taken directly from hands-on experience gathered over many years by Amy Strausser, Master Gardener.

Definitions of words marked with an * can be found in the glossary.

Be aware that seeds cannot be purchased out of season in many local stores. Most are collected by distributors by the end of the growing season. Sale of seed packets begins in stores in January. You may purchase seeds out of season on line at www.seedman.com.

About the Author

Gardening has been a wonderful hobby for me. I have loved digging in the dirt since childhood. It was great fun following my father around our garden at home in West Virginia. Barefoot and fascinated, I'd shadow him through the rows of newly sprouted corn and beans. He taught me how to hoe and weed and best of all to love the wonders of creation. It became pure joy working the earth and watching each spring as a new crop emerged. And for our hard work we gained a great feeling of accomplishment at harvest time. Warm dirt between the toes and the fresh smells of spring still get me excited and remind me of the delights of working together with my dad on warm summer days.

But there is something that gets me even more excited than gardening. It's the way in which God has worked in my life. I became a Christian at the age of nine. I knew that my mother and father were Christians and were going to be with God in heaven. I also knew that I could not be a Christian just because they were. I had to decide for myself that Jesus had died for me personally. Since inviting Jesus into my heart, God has blessed me in so many ways. He has given me strength in times of weakness, and has demonstrated over and over again his love and mercy toward me. I have learned that God is with me through hardship, sometimes even carrying me through difficult circumstances. He is true to his Word and is faithful to show me his power in my life. I have grown to understand that obedience to his Word brings great peace and joy. And I have learned that I am happiest when I am in the center of his will. A deep personal peace comes from meeting God each new day and by spending time talking with him and reading his Word. Each time I reread Scripture I find it reaches out to meet my specific needs. The peace I find in studying his Word allows me to place my fears and worries down at his feet and live in the joy he intended for me from the beginning.

So it's quite natural to blend my love of gardening with my love for God. He has given us so many examples in his Word that have to do with man and the soil. Right from the very beginning of creation he situated Adam and Eve in a beautiful garden, surrounded by plants, trees, and animals.

I invite you as a new Christian to begin to learn all that God can be in your life. Prepare to grow in his power, and as you grow spiritually, learn about his creation, our life-sustaining earth.

Begin a real garden along with this study and see how the life of a plant and the life of a new and growing Christian parallel each other in so many ways. Once you've discovered how similar the two are, you will never again garden without thinking of the life lessons learned in this study. Applications will come to mind each time you plant something and nurture it to maturity.

Preface

New life begins at the point of recognition of Christ as Savior and Lord. Our righteousness is obtained from his shed blood for our sins. Scripture says, ". . . that while we were yet sinners Christ died for us. His sacrifice for us purifies us and makes us acceptable in God's sight." Thus, we begin a new relationship with our heavenly Father who loves us and wants to bring us to new life and strength by his power. John 3:16 says, "For God so loved the world that he gave his one and only Son, that who ever believes in him shall not perish but have eternal life." Believing that Jesus is God's son is not enough. Jesus came to bring the free gift of salvation. That was his full purpose.

The Christian journey begins at the foot of the cross, where we can receive Jesus as Savior, ask for forgiveness, and turn from our past as we grow and learn, trust and obey, and mature to fullness of joy. Here we begin to understand and accept God's will and purpose for our individual lives. We realize that we cannot live our lives in our own strength with any degree of success. We begin to depend on God and his promised faithfulness to us.

He said, "I will never leave you nor forsake you. Come unto me all you who are weary and heavy laden and I will give you rest." Jesus said, "Take my yoke upon you and learn from me, for I am gentle and humble in heart, and you will find rest for your souls. For my yoke is easy and my burden is light." Here he invites us to lean on him and learn about him; a life-long journey.

I challenge you as you go through this study to do the gardening activities so that you can see two things:

1. How stages of seed and plant development mirror stages of Christian growth.
2. How daily gardening and cultivation parallel daily exercise and discipline as you mature in your spiritual growth.

Take time now to pray that God will reveal his truth to you and that your feet (roots) will be planted in his Word as you learn ways to become a mature Christian, attaining to the whole measure of the fullness of Christ.

I pray that each of you has come to a belief and acceptance of Jesus as Savior and that you are prepared to be firmly planted and growing.

If you have never received Jesus as your Lord and Savior, I invite you to do so. Asking him to come in is as easy as praying this prayer: Dear Lord Jesus, I ask you to come into my heart. I know that I am a sinner and I need you to save me from my sins. Teach me how to live and grow; be my guide and friend forever. Amen.

If you have just prayed this prayer, then let me be the first to congratulate you and welcome you into the family of God. May your heart be filled with excitement as you grow and discover the joy of your salvation.

Let's Get Growing!
Biblical Description of a
Mature Christian

In the New Testament we see an excellent word picture describing mature Christian character.

11 It was he who gave some to be apostles, some to be prophets, some to be evangelists, and some to be pastors and teachers 12 to prepare God's people for works of service, so that the body of Christ may be built up 13 until we all reach unity in the faith and in the knowledge of the Son of God and become mature, attaining to the whole measure of the fullness of Christ. 14 Then we will no longer be infants, tossed back and forth by the waves, and blown here and there by every wind of teaching and by the cunning and craftiness of men in their deceitful scheming. 15 From him the whole body joined and held together by every support-

ing ligament, grows and builds itself up in love, as
each part does its work. (Ephesians 4:11–15)

God has revealed his blueprint for our growth
to maturity. We are to be strong and firmly planted
in him. We are as functioning plants in God's garden. He has put us here for fellowship with him, to
evolve from babies into mature active Christian men
and women gaining wisdom and producing fruit for
his glory. God supplies us with the proper growth
stimuli to perform remarkable things to glorify him.

Blessed is the man you *discipline*, Oh Lord, the man
you *teach* from your law; you grant him relief from
days of trouble . . . Obedience to his teachings
brings a whole host of blessings. (Psalm 94:12)

Blessed is the man who perseveres under trial, because when he has stood the test, he will receive
the crown of life that God has promised to those
who love him. (James 1:12)

These passages of Scripture are chock-full of information about God's plan for believers. They
spell out the importance of knowing and obeying
God and list warnings we will want to heed, and
traps to look for. We will address all these things in
this study.

The Parable of the Seed

Jesus used allegories, called parables, with familiar subjects to help his followers understand his message.

Let's begin by reading the Parable of the Seed.

That same day Jesus went out of the house and sat by the lake. 2 Such large crowds gathered around him that he got into a boat and sat in it, while all the people stood on the shore. 3 Then he told them many things in parables, saying: "A farmer went out to sow his seed. 4 as he was scattering the seed, some fell along the path, and the birds came and ate it up. 5 Some fell on rocky places, where it did not have much soil. It sprang up quickly, because the soil was shallow. 6 But when the sun came up, the plants were scorched, and they withered because they had no root. 7 Other seed fell among thorns, which grew up and choked the plants. 8 Still other seed fell on good soil, where it produced a crop—a hundred, sixty or thirty times what was sown. 9 He who has ears, let him hear. (Matthew 13:1–9)

The parables Jesus used were understood by those who were seeking earnestly, but they often baffled casual observers. Jesus may have meant it to be that way so that those who would oppose him or who were overzealous could not steer his ministry to an untimely end.

Jesus explains this parable in Matthew 13:18–23.

Listen to what the parable of the sower means: 19 When anyone hears the message about the kingdom and does not understand it, the evil one comes and snatches away what was sown in his heart. This is the seed sown along the path. 20 The one who received the seed that fell on rocky places is the man who hears the word and at once receives it with joy. 21 But since he has no root, he lasts only a short time. When trouble or persecution comes because of the word, he quickly falls away. 22 The one who received the seed that fell among the thorns is the man who hears the word, but the worries of this life and the deceitfulness of wealth choke it, making it unfruitful. 23 But the one who received the seed that fell on good soil is the man who hears the word and understands it. He produces a crop, yielding a hundred, sixty or thirty times what was sown.

There are some essential factors to consider for good growth with both Christians and plants. Let's begin as gardeners do by determining the location for starting a successful garden.

Gardener's Beginning

When a gardener decides to start a new planting, he first decides on the location for his planting. For this study we are going to plant in FULL SON. In John 8:12 Jesus spoke to them, saying, "I am the light of the world. Whoever follows me will never walk in darkness, but have the light of life." Light is one of the essentials for the life and growth of every plant and child of God. Light aids plant function, so we are going to begin in a Son-lit spot. For our plant-Christian comparison, we will be using a man and a zinnia. If you don't have a place outside to plant a garden, don't give up. Everyone will start their seeds inside. Indoor gardeners will plant parsley, basil, thyme, or dill seeds. Patio gardeners can use zinnia or patio tomato seeds. (All these seeds are chosen because they are relatively easy to start.)

Those with garden plots will transplant their seedlings to that site. Patio gardeners will transplant their seedlings to pots. Indoor gardeners can transplant to pots for the windowsill, or for under grow lights.*

A C T I V I T Y # 1

It Is Time for a Stroll

Take a walk in your yard and look for a place to start a garden. For this study, you will want to choose a site that is in the sun most of the day. If you will be gardening inside or on your patio instead, you may want to spend this time preparing a place in a sun-lit window. You might obtain a plant stand that will hold the plants you will grow in the coming lessons, or purchase pots with good drainage for your patio area. Be sure you get pots that have saucers too. They are the best for your plants because they allow the soil to maintain a good rate of moisture. Don't become discouraged, there are lots of ways to grow plants successfully. Don't worry about the size of your garden yet. We'll cover that in coming chapters.

WHEN AND HOW DOES GROWTH BEGIN?

A Christ follower, one who has received Jesus as Savior, begins to cultivate a new life. God gives us the right and privilege to call on him for help.

> Yet to all who received him, to those who believed in his name, he gave the right to become children of God. As his children we have all the rights and privileges of sons and daughters. We are heirs to all that the father has. (John 1:12)

> Now if we are children, then we are heirs-heirs of God and coheirs with Christ, if indeed we share in his sufferings in order that we may also share in his glory. (Romans 8:17)

> And you also were included in Christ when you heard the word of truth, the gospel of your salvation. Having believed, you were marked in him with a seal, the promised Holy Spirit, who is a deposit guaranteeing our inheritance until the redemption of those who are God's possession, to the praise of his glory. (Ephesians 1:13–14)

We nurture our newfound faith the same way we care for a plant. This study will teach you what is necessary to keep yourself healthy and vital as you grow in Christ.

God's message is heard by many different kinds of people in many different places. Some understand

and accept it and some are not yet ready. Those who accept his message recognize their sin, turn away from it, and become children of God.

> Repent and be baptized, every one of you, in the name of Jesus Christ for the forgiveness of your sins. And you will receive the gift of the Holy Spirit. (Acts 2:38)

God calls his children and if they come to him, repent, and believe, they are made ready to grow by the indwelling of the Holy Spirit. We will see in this chapter just how the Holy Spirit works in us.

FIRST, LET'S LOOK AT THE MEANING OF REPENTANCE

It is the most important part of your new life in Christ. As you come to him, you need to ask forgiveness for your past sins and then make a conscious change in direction, a deliberate turn from the past toward a future following Jesus' example. You turn a corner from sin to salvation. I like to think of it as turning a corner, because in doing so you can't see what you have left behind. As you ask for forgiveness, be assured that God no longer sees your sins. They are covered by the blood of our Savior and Lord.

> He does not treat us as our sins deserve or repay us according to our iniquities. 11 For as high as the heavens are above the earth, so great is his love

31

for those who fear him; 12 as far as the east is from
the west, so far has he removed our transgressions
from us. (Psalm 103:10–12)

Once you've turned the corner, train your eyes
on what lies ahead: God's plan for your life, a blessed
future. For Christ's love compels us, because we are
convinced that one died for all, and therefore all
died.

15 And he died for all, that those who live should
no longer live for themselves but for him who died
for them and was raised again. (2 Corinthians
5:14–15)

When Jesus died, he was buried, and on the third
day, as he had promised, he rose again. He demonstrated his power over death. He then showed himself to his followers for the next forty days. Finally,
he gathered his disciples about him and explained
to them that he would ascend to his father, but would
send the comforter, the Holy Spirit, to be with them.

1. Once you have become a Christian and realize that your sins are forgiven, what should
    be your reason for doing good things?

    _____

    _____

    _____

2.   Before you became a Christian, what was
     your motivation for doing good things?

_____

_____

_____

THE HOLY SPIRIT, OUR COMFORT AND HELP

In Ephesians, Paul writes: "Now as sons of God we
may approach his throne, seek his face and make
our requests known to him." Praying, asking, and
learning from him. Through Christ, we may approach God with freedom and confidence.

> For this reason I kneel before the Father. 15 from
> whom his whole family in heaven and on earth
> derives its name. 16 I pray that out of his glorious
> riches he may strengthen you with power through
> his Spirit in your inner being. 17 so that Christ
> may dwell in your hearts through faith, And I pray
> that you, being *rooted and established* in love, 18
> may have power, together with all the saints, to
> grasp how wide and long and high and deep is the
> love of Christ, 19 and to know this love that sur-
> passes knowledge—that you may be filled to the
> measure of all the fullness of God. (Ephesians
> 3:14–19)

The dictionary defines the word *established* this way:

> to make steadfast, firm, or stable, to settle on a firm or permanent basis; to set or fix unalterably, to enact or decree authoritatively and for permanence, to ordain, to strengthen, to prove and secure the permanent existence of.

3.   What are the things Paul prays for?

_____

_____

_____

4.   What is meant by the fullness of God?

_____

_____

_____

The Spirit searches all things, even the deep things of God. 11 For who among men knows the thoughts of a man except the man's spirit within him? In the same way no one knows the thoughts of God except the Spirit of God. 12 We have not received the spirit of the world but the Spirit who is from God, that we may understand what God has freely given us. 13 This is what we speak, not in words taught us by human wisdom but in words taught by the Spirit, expressing spiritual truths in spiritual words. 14 The man without the Spirit does not accept the things that come from the Spirit of God, for they are foolishness to him, and he cannot understand them, because they are spiritually discerned. (1 Corinthians 2:10–14)

5.　Who knows God's thoughts?

_____

_____

_____

6.　How then are we to understand what God wants for us?

_____

_____

_____

7.　Who does not accept the things that come from the Spirit of God?

_____

_____

_____

8. What do Spirit-filled things seem like to the
    man without the Spirit?

_____

_____

_____

9. Think about the word *established*. How does
    the dictionary meaning help us understand
    our establishment by God?

_____

_____

_____

TRANSFORMED NOT CONFORMED

All people on earth conform to the world in some
ways. We conform to the world by following the
laws of the land. We conform when we join a sports
team, the army, or by wearing certain identifiable
clothing. Even in our churches we conform to par-

ticular religious rites proposed by that certain denomination, such as the different ways services are conducted. While conformity is appropriate in many cases, we must be careful that it does not hinder or take the place of our inward transformation that was begun in the Spirit. Our appearance in church on Sunday should not be our only demonstration of faith in God.

> Do not conform any longer to the pattern of this world, but be transformed by the renewing of your mind. Then you will be able to test and approve what God's will is—his good, pleasing and perfect will. (Romans 12:2)

10. What does renewing of the mind do to transform us?

_____

_____

_____

By faith we begin to grow in our spiritual walk. We make deliberate choices to embrace faith in God, and invite him to sit, as it were, in the driver's seat of our lives. Transformation begins and we are changed on the inside. Where there was fear, it is replaced with peace. Where there was hate, love now lives. Selfishness is replaced with a giving spirit. We are transformed into the likeness of Christ. The progression of growth begins in our being broken at the foot of the cross. We, in a sense, are torn down to be rebuilt for victory in him.

The apostle Paul wrote this while in prison: "I have learned to be content whatever the circumstances" (Philippians 4:11).

His deeply personal relationship with the risen Lord transformed him, renewed his mind, and gave him a peace that passed all understanding. In Paul's case, his transformation gave him the very strength he needed to conform to and endure long periods of time in prison.

WHY DO GOD'S WILL?

Our faith in Christ compels us to action for God's glory. Faith is the foundation for all that we believe about our heavenly Father. He asks us to put our faith in him even though we have not seen him face to face. He asks us to exercise our faith in him and live out that faith, daily trusting him.

Let's look at four of the characteristics of God that we can claim as trustworthy foundations for a faith in him.

FAITH IN GOD'S WISDOM

But God made the earth by his power; he founded the world by his wisdom and stretched out the heavens by his understanding. (Jeremiah 10:12)

This passage reminds us of the wisdom of our creator. He, who made everything that we know, has fathomless wisdom. We can put our faith in his wisdom, because he knows all things.

FAITH IN GOD'S GOODNESS

"For I know the plans I have for you," declares the Lord, "plans to prosper you and not to harm you, plans to give you hope and a future." (Jeremiah 29:11)

Isn't it wonderful to know that the God we serve intends the very best for us? He has known us from the very beginning, and has made hope-filled plans for us, for now, and the future.

FAITH IN HIS POWER

I keep asking that the God of our Lord Jesus Christ, the glorious Father, may give you the Spirit of wisdom and revelation, so that you may know him better. 18 I pray also that the eyes of your heart may be enlightened in order that you may know the hope to which he has called you. The riches of his glorious inheritance in the saints, 19 and his incomparably great power for us who believe. That power is like the working of his mighty strength, 20 which he exerted in Christ when he raised him from the dead and seated him at his right hand in the heavenly realms, 21 far above all rule and authority, power and dominion, and every title that can be given, not only in the present age but also in the one to come. (Ephesians 1:17–21)

Truly, there is no power in heaven or on earth like God's. We can put our whole faith in him because he has offered his power to us through our believing in his son Jesus Christ.

FAITH IN GOD'S FAITHFULNESS

Now I am about to go the way of all the earth. You know with all your heart and soul that not one of the good promises the Lord your God gave you has failed. Every promise has been fulfilled; not one has failed. (Joshua 23:14)

God keeps his promise to be faithful. He will never leave us or forsake us. We can put our full trust in his Word because he keeps his word. Therefore, with a strong faith in such an awesome God, we may strike out on this journey with all confidence.

A C T I V I T Y   #   2

Choosing a Spot for a Real Garden

This process will need to be done approximately two weeks before the last frost date in your region, if you are going to start an outdoor garden at the earliest spring date. More information regarding that date will be found at the end of this section. Outdoor gardeners may begin their garden anytime during April, May, and June if this is after the frost date in your locale.

For our new garden, we are going to choose a site in full sun. If you are a beginning gardener, don't prepare a very large area. Gradually, as you gain experience, you can enlarge your garden plot. Keep it manageable, according to the time you have to spend. I advise a very small area if you work five days a week outside your home. Then you will be able to maintain and enjoy it. An easy garden to maintain will be in a range of five to six feet long and three to four feet front to back. This will keep down your costs for equipment, fertilizer, and water. If you find you don't have time, or a green thumb, you haven't spent an enormous amount of money on items you won't use in the future. Clear the area of grass, weeds, and stone. Turn the soil over with a spade or tiller to a depth of ten to twelve inches. You should be able to sift the soil through your fingers, but it should not be powder fine. Soil that is powder fine, when moistened, will not let air reach plant roots. Roots will then begin to rot and the plants will die.

To ensure good growth, you should test the soil in your garden and amend it as needed. You can call your local nurseryman for information regarding soil in your area. Or you can use the test that appears later in this text. (See *Fertile Soil.*) Your garden should be ready for planting a week before the predicted last frost date in your area. Your local landscaper will know that approximate date or you can access your county agricultural extension web site, or reach them by phone. If you are gardening on the patio or windowsill, purchase potting soil from your local garden shop. Some premixed soil has the first dose of fertilizer in it.

Purchase seeds recommended in the section called, *Gardener's Beginnings.*

SMART SEEDS!

It is amazing to note that even a tiny seed knows which way is up. Studies on plants, carried out in space, reveal that even a small seedling (cotyledon*) knows that its roots grow down in the soil and the stem grows in the opposite direction, toward the light. The light draws the plant toward growth stimuli and finally, maturity and fruiting.

For a moment consider the tiny seed. It is very small, dry, and hard. On the outside it is much like any grain of sand or dried particle of wood, but its potential is nothing less than amazing! A tiny mustard seed can produce a huge plant! God can take the least and most insignificant man and make him into a powerful instrument for his glory. We will learn what increases our potential as new believers as we continue this study.

GOOD SOIL

Soil preparation is very important to the basic success of each new plant or Christian. As we have already read, we will need good soil.

God tells us in his Word that we will grow only if we sink our roots into his Word.

So then, just as you received Christ Jesus as Lord, continue to live in him, 7 rooted and built up in him, strengthened in the faith as you were taught, and overflowing with thankfulness. (Colossians 2:6–7)

11. What length of time does the word *continue* imply in verse six?

_____

_____

_____

Jesus describes the different growth problems of different kinds of sites and soils. Read again the parable of the sower, as found this time in Luke. Highlight the qualities of good soil.

While a large crowd was gathering and people were coming to Jesus from town after town, he told this parable: 5 "A farmer went out to sow his seed. As he was scattering the seed, some fell along the path; it was trampled on, and the birds of the air ate it up. 6 Some fell on rock and when it came up, the plants withered because they had no moisture. 7 Other seed fell among thorns, which grew up with it and choked the plants. 8 Still other seed fell on good soil. It came up and yielded a crop, a hundred times more than was sown." When he said this, he called out, "He who has ears to hear, let him hear." 9 His disciples asked him what this parable meant. 10 He said, "The knowledge of the secrets of the kingdom of God has been given to you, but to others I speak in parables, so that, "though seeing, they may not see; though hearing, they may not understand. 11 "This is the meaning of the parable: The seed is the word of God. 12 Those along the path are the ones who hear, and then the devil comes and takes away the word from their hearts, so that they may not believe and be saved. 13 Those on the rock are the ones who received the word with joy when they hear it, but they have no root. They believe for a while, but in the time of testing they fall away. 14 The seed that fell among thorns stands for those who hear, but as they go on their way they are choked by life's worries, riches and pleasures, and they do not mature. 15 But the seed on good soil stands for those with a noble and good heart, who hear the word, retain it, and by persevering produce a crop. (Luke 8:4–15)

12. Look up the word *noble* in the dictionary and write the definition here.

_____

_____

_____

45

13. What are the characteristics of the person who accepts the Word?

_____

_____

_____

The definition of *persevering*: steady persistence in a course of action, a purpose, a state. Synonyms: doggedness, steadfastness. Perseverance commonly suggests activity maintained in spite of difficulties—steadfast and a long, continued application.

Regarding perseverance:

> And we rejoice in the hope of the glory of God. 3 Not only so; but we also rejoice in our sufferings, because we know that suffering produces perseverance; 4 perseverance, character; and character, hope. 5 And hope does not disappoint us, because God has poured out his love into our hearts by the Holy Spirit, whom he has given us. (Romans 5:2b–5)

Notice that we are to rejoice in our sufferings. Rejoice in spite of the suffering and rejoice that suffering will produce perseverance and finally, hope. Rejoice because you can access God's power to overcome difficult times. Suffering can be spiritual, emotional, or physical.

14. Look closely at the meaning of perseverance. Notice that the dictionary meaning includes the words *long, continued application*
What are the implications for the Christian?

_____

_____

_____

15. If you are suffering from something in your
life today, write it here. Pray about it now
and ask God help you see his presence
through this time.

_____

_____

_____

PLANTS STARTED INDOORS

Now that we have seen that good soil is important
to the success of our spiritual seeds, let's take a look
at the importance of good soil to the seeds you will
plant. The smallest seed, when placed in the right
site and soil and with stimulation, will begin to open
and send down tender roots. Therefore, the soil must
be prepared properly.

Plants will be healthiest if started in good soil. You can minimize ninety percent of plant problems by planting in good soil.

What makes up good, loamy soil? A combination of twenty percent air, forty-five percent minerals, five percent organic material, and thirty percent water. Air allows room for roots to grow. Minerals like sand, silt, and clay give some nutrients, drainage, and texture. Organic material, such as decaying matter (plants, animals, microbes) add nutrients to the mixture.

SOIL TEST

Moisten a small amount of soil to the consistency of putty. Roll it into a half-inch diameter ball. Press the ball. If the ball breaks apart, the soil is sandy. Clay can be worked to form a ribbon of soil. Loam, which contains approximately equal volumes of sand, silt, and clay particles, will stick together when pressed, but will not form a ribbon of more than half an inch in length.

Patio and window gardeners can relax here. When you buy the premixed soil at the garden shop, be assured that the manufacturers have added the proper elements.

ACTIVITY # 3

Starting Seeds

Start your seeds in starter trays. (Cost is about $3.00 each.) In this way you can get a jump on the growing season and save money too! You may purchase these from the garden department of your local store, or you can use small containers from home. You can use your starter trays year after year. Each cell or container must hold half a cup of soil and have a drainage hole at the bottom. Yogurt containers work well. You may make holes in the bottom of the yogurt container with a quarter-inch drill bit or, punch multiple holes with an ice pick or awl. Purchase seed starter soil mixture, a product perfected for starting seeds which eliminates messy measuring and mixing. Fill each cell to the top with starter mix so that emerging seedlings can receive good airflow near the roots.

Water is essential in the first phase of germination. Water penetrates the seed coat and causes the endosperm to swell. The seed coat, softened by water, splits open as the endosperm swells. The water dissolves nutrients in the endosperm, making them available to the embryo, and growth begins. The growing medium must be constantly moist, but not soggy. Conversely, if seeds are allowed to go dry, they will not germinate.

After you have filled each cell with planting medium, dampen the soil. Plant no more than three seeds to a cell, to avoid crowding. (You don't have to plant all the seeds. You can place the remaining seeds in a closed jar and put it in the crisper drawer of your refrigerator. Most seeds will be viable for a year or two if stored this way.) Place all containers on a tray and slip into a clear garbage bag and close with a twist tie. If you are using a commercial starter tray, follow the instructions and cover with the clear lid provided. Place your covered tray in a warm sunny window; seedlings should begin to erupt in a few days to two weeks, depending on the type of seed. Or you may want to place your starter trays under a grow light.* However, grow lights do not supply the same warmth as the sun provides. You may want to provide warmth by placing a heating coil under your trays. These coils can be purchased at a garden shop. You might try placing a small lamp with a 60-watt bulb directly under your seed trays. The lamp must remain on the entire time till your seedlings erupt through the soil.

After seedlings erupt, remove warming devices and the plastic cover or plastic bag. Keep plants at room temperature. Air must flow over the plants to prevent damping off. Damping off* will occur when there is too much moisture. A fungus can attack the plants and cause them to die.

Move plant trays to an area lit only with a grow light.* This will keep your plants low and compact and increase sturdiness. If a grow light is not used, plants will become too tall and spindly. Growing plants will need seventeen to eighteen hours of light each day. Keep the light four to five inches away from the tops of the plants; as they grow, move the light to maintain that same distance.

A grow light is simply florescent tube lighting like those sometimes used in the workshop or garage. (Cost is about $10 for the light which can be purchased at any home supply store. Bulbs will be extra. One warm-white, 40-watt bulb and one coolwhite, 40-watt bulb used together are adequate for seed starting and seedling growth. Special grow lights are also suitable, but more expensive.)

Water all seedlings from below by pouring water in the holding tray beneath individual cells or containers. The soil will draw the water up through the holes in the bottom of the container. Watering from above can cause tender plants to lie flat on the soil and impede growth. If you want to moisten the soil on top, use a spray bottle filled with tap water.

IN THE SON

Read again John 8:12: "When Jesus spoke again to the people, he said, 'I am the light of the world. Whoever follows me will never walk in darkness, but will have the light of life.'" Like the constant, close light on our new seedlings, we need the close and constant light of Christ in our lives.

As Christians we grow in the Son, and for the Son. He bathes us in his light and gives us our energy to live and grow spiritually.

> When Jesus spoke again to the people, he said, "I am the light of the world. Whoever follows me will never walk in darkness, but will have the light of life." (John 8:12)

> In the beginning was the Word, and the Word was with God, and the Word was God. He was with God in the beginning. Through him all things were made; without him nothing was made that has been made. In him was life, and that life was the light of men. (John 1:1–4)

Growing in Christ is a life-long project. He never stops asking us to grow and change.

16. How has God asked you to grow and change lately? Explain

Sun is as important as water for the successful growth of plants. The warmth and energy expended by our sun generate growth. Each plant that grows goes through a process known as photosynthesis*. Photosynthesis is the process by which light energy is utilized to convert carbon dioxide and water into food to be used by plants. Oxygen is released into the air during the process. Light of solar energy is captured by chlorophyll (the green pigment in leaves). It is then converted into chemical energy that is stored as starch or sugar. These starches and sugars are stored in roots, stems, and fruits. They are available to the plant as food or fuel. Plants differ from animals in that animals cannot manufacture their own food from light energy. The word *photosynthesis* means *to put together with light*.

Above we learned about the growth of a plant and the process of photosynthesis.

Growth as a Christian works the same way. As a Christ follower grows, he begins to change his look. He is spiritually stronger, sturdier, and more able to cope with the challenges of life. As a Christian grows he should start to resemble Christ and continue to live in the Son. Maybe we should start calling this process *Sonsynthesis*. This is the activity of taking

53

in the living water, respiration through confession, prayer, and studying God's Word, which in turn sends food to the soul, which sends out more roots to hold a believer firmly in place as Sonsynthesis continues on and on.

> No longer are we infants, tossed back and forth by the waves, and blown here and there by every wind of teaching and by the cunning and craftiness of men in their deceitful scheming. 15 Instead, speaking the truth in love, we will in all things grow up into him who is the head, that is, Christ. 16 From him the whole body, joined and held together by every supporting ligament, grows and builds itself up in love, as each part does its work. Our physical bodies have many parts that help the whole. We need each part. Our eyes cannot do the work of our hands. Our feet cannot do the work of our ears. Each part of our body is important to the whole body. (Ephesians 4:14–16)

So the church needs many parts working together to make it grow. The church needs pastors, teachers, leaders, and office workers, those who minister to the needs of others. Churches need janitors, grounds keepers, and treasurers. In the lifetime of a Christian, one may experience God's calling to different jobs along the way. He may ask a teacher to leave that role and become a minister to the elderly, or head a building project, or become a short— or long-term missionary. We can have several roles in a lifetime and each can strengthen us as believers.

The basic theme is always to grow in the love and knowledge of Christ and do his will.

17. a. How might a person grow by doing a job that takes him out of his comfort zone?

_____

_____

_____

b. What are some things one might expect to see God doing during this time?

_____

_____

_____

18. How do you think God might use your unique abilities in the church to help you and others grow in Christ?

_____

_____

_____

GOD'S POWER AND THE LIGHT OF LIFE
SOMETHING TO THINK ABOUT

Sit in the direct rays of the sun on a hot day. Feel the sun on your face; its heat and even its light can be unbearably intense. Now think of the sun's effect on the earth. Without its heat and life-giving effects, plants would not be able to grow. The power of the heat and light from the sun is immense, essential for life on our planet. Without the sun, scientists say our world would grow cold and die. We could not live without it. And if it were closer to the earth, its heat would consume everything on our planet.

As you experience the hot sun on you and you sense the life abounding about you—the warm air, the animal life, the plant life—you get a glimpse of the power of our living God. He created all that we see and know, including the sun itself. It warms our planet and sustains life, and has power far surpassing mortal man's imagination. Writers of the Old Testament attempted to explain God's unspeakable potency. We see in the twenty-fourth chapter of Exodus a verbal description of the glory of the Lord; "Then Moses went up the mountain and disappeared into the cloud at the top. And the glory of the Lord rested upon Mount Sinai and the cloud covered it six days. The seventh day he called to Moses from the cloud." Those at the bottom of the mountain saw the awesome sight; the glory of the Lord on the mountaintop looked like a raging fire. And Moses disappeared into the cloud-covered mountaintop.

Have you ever been near a raging fire and felt its unbearable heat? Now imagine walking into that inferno as Moses did. What gave him the ability to enter that gloriously lit place of meeting? Only God can answer that question. He enabled Moses to survive being in his powerful presence. Others below, too frightened, begged Moses to talk to God for them for fear they would die from the experience.

If the sun perched millions of miles away is too magnificent for us to bear for more than a few hours at our present distance, think what standing in God's powerful presence will be like. He who appointed the sun's position in space and with his mouth spoke its duties, embodies the ultimate glorious power. Man's inability to grasp the incalculable power of God is evident, but we can make an attempt by comparing him to the sun, his handiwork. His glorious power far exceeds our understanding.

In the book of Revelation, John was given the words to open man's eyes to what we might behold when we are made witnesses to God's full glory. He described heaven in terms that we can understand, a crystal sea, things made of gold and precious stone. These are things we know and understand. But what does heaven hold for us? We can't even imagine. If we are unable to withstand the heat and light of the sun, how much will we need to be changed to stand in his presence?

When we seek his presence, he asks for one prerequisite, that we are covered with the blood of Jesus by which we are made perfect to stand at the foot of his throne. He makes a way for us to come to him. God came in the form of a man, Jesus, to show us many things. As Jesus healed the sick, fed the hungry, and taught valuable life lessons of obedience to God's laws, we were able to see his unconditional love for the least and the worst of mankind. As he teaches about his forgiveness and love, he invites us to come to him, desiring a close fellowship, like father and son/daughter. God demonstrated his power and love in the person of Jesus Christ. He took on himself the sins of the entire world, past, present and future, to redeem us. We cannot imagine the strength it took for Christ to bear that cruel burden for our soul's sake, but in doing so, he brought the light of life to all mankind.

MORE ABOUT WATER

Read the story of everlasting water as told by the apostle John.

> Now he had to go through Samaria. 5 So he came to a town in Samaria called Sychar, near the plot of ground Jacob had given to his son Joseph. 6 Jacob's well was there, and Jesus, tired as he was from the journey, sat down by the well. It was about

the sixth hour. 7 When a Samaritan woman came to draw water, Jesus said to her, "Will you give me a drink?" 8 (His disciples had gone into the town to buy food.) 9 The Samaritan woman said to him, "you are a Jew and I am a Samaritan woman. How can you ask me for a drink?" (For Jews do not associate with Samaritans.) 10 Jesus answered her, "If you knew the gift of God and who it is that asks you for a drink, you would have asked him and he would have given you living water." 11 "Sir," the woman said, "you have nothing to draw with and the well is deep, Where can you get this living water? 12 Are you greater than our father Jacob, who gave us the well and drank from it himself, as did also his sons and his flocks and herds?" 13 Jesus answered, "Everyone who drinks this water will be thirsty again, 14 But whoever drinks the water I give him will never thirst. Indeed, the water I give him will become in him a spring of water welling up to eternal life." (John 4:4–14)

19. What does Jesus, the living water, promise those who receive Him?

_____

_____

_____

We find these words in John 7:37–38.

On the last and greatest day of the feast, Jesus stood and said in a loud voice, "If anyone is thirsty, let him come to me and drink. 38 Whoever believes in me, as the Scripture has said, streams of living water will flow from within him." Here again we see the importance of life-giving water to the growing Christian.

TAPPING INTO THE LIVING WATER ON A DAILY BASIS

The new Christian begins to grow by developing a knowledge of who God is. He tells us that we are to seek his face and learn about him. God speaks to us and answers our requests when we take the time to pray and listen to him. We rob ourselves of valuable fellowship with him, if we aren't talking to him, worshiping him, and asking for his help. What can we know of him if we do not talk with him and read his Word? We must stay in God's Word and be fed and watered. If we stay in his will, we will grow strong and be useful.

This is the confidence we have in approaching God: that if we ask anything according to his will, he hears us. 15 and if we know that he hears us—whatever we ask—we know that we have what we asked of him. (1 John 5:14–15)

How many of us live our lives saying, today I will _____ (fill in the blank). Rather than saying,

"First we must seek God and then do what he would have us do," we manage to fit God into the little pockets of our lives that are left after we do what we want. God wants to be first in our lives and when we put him first we see a whole different life, the abundant life that he has for us. In the book of Matthew, Jesus taught his followers not to worry about what they would eat or wear, for pagans run after these things. God knows that you need these things.

> Seek first his kingdom and his righteousness, and all these things will be given to you as well. (Matthew 6:33)

SPIRITUAL DISCIPLINES THAT HELP US TAP INTO THE WELL AND INCREASE OUR POTENTIAL
TRAINING YOUR CHARACTER

Man's natural character is sinful. Roman 3:23 says, "For every man has sinned and come short of the glory of God." We are products of our sinful nature. Adam and Eve sinned in the Garden of Eden and passed that sinful nature on to all mankind. Their disobedience to God brought about their separation from him because he cannot look on sin. God then required the blood of an animal as atonement for man's sin. Later, he sent his only son Jesus Christ to shed his blood once and for all for man. Belief in Jesus as Savior brings us back into God's favor so that we may experience the blessings of God and eternal life.

Psalm 8:3–6 speaks of our Father's creation of us. David writes:

> When I consider your heavens, the works of your fingers, the moon and the stars, which you have set in place, what is man that you are mindful of him, the son of man, that you care for him? You made him a little lower than the heavenly beings and crowned him with glory and honor. You made him ruler over the works of your hands; you put everything under his feet.

20. Describe in your own words the characteristics God gave mankind.

_____

_____

_____

21. How should we apply these characteristics to our lives today?

_____

_____

_____

Then God said, "Let us make man in our image, in our likeness, and let them rule over the fish of the sea and the birds of the air, over the livestock, over all earth, and over all the creatures that move along the ground." 27 So God created man in his own image, in the image of God he created him; male and female he created them. (Genesis 1:26–27)

22. What did God place in man's care?

_____

_____

_____

23. Does this give us a glimpse of the great things God planned for man? Explain.

_____

_____

_____

24. Who is *us* in verse 26?

_____

_____

_____

It is only human nature to want to belong to someone or something. Finding out who we are and where we belong in this world is vitally important. God tells us in his Word that we are his and he is ours. We are his children and he is our Father. Every man, woman, and child was made in his image and for a relationship with him. How wonderful it is to belong to such a loving Father, one who has made us like him, to live with him and to love him. Each of us is special to him because he has made each of us. As Christians, we are members of a huge family, and yet, are individual and unique. God has made each of us especially for a purpose, and as we learn about him, we begin to see his plan for us unfold. What a blessing it is for God to reveal to us our intended purpose as we study and put into practice, his Word, the Holy Bible. There is no greater satisfaction than to know your purpose for living and to be active in that purpose.

The Christian walk begins with knowledge of the Father, and the Christian begins to grow and mature by exercising and practicing what he or she learns. Some have defined wisdom as knowledge in action. King Solomon, one of the wisest kings of ancient Israel, wrote in Proverbs 2:6, "For the Lord gives wisdom, and from his mouth come knowledge and understanding."

Stop now and ask God for understanding and wisdom. That is what he wants for us. He will be faithful to give it if we ask him for it.

Like the marathon runner, who practices running every day, eats proper food, and gets proper rest so that he might be successful in the race, we as Christians must practice and train through discipline. We should not pray fervently for a miracle from God because we think that practicing our discipline is too time consuming. We must not be like the man who prayed, "Lord give me patience and give it to me now." We must practice patience daily, along with self-control, peace, joy, and other fruits of the spirit so that when we need them the most, they automatically occur.

For instance, each of us has things that make us really angry. God calls us to exhibit self-control. That means we are not responsible for anyone else but ourselves. We are not responsible for the one who makes us angry, but we are responsible for our anger. Looking at oneself and making adjustments can be very intimidating. In doing so, we must first admit the sin, and secondly, take personal responsibility for it. If we shy away from that fundamental work, our process of growth slows considerably.

Again, like the runner, we must practice, practice, practice, and practice some more. The disciplined Christian will grow in the experience and be useful, readily recognizing the Father's voice. The need for extensive practice of a given discipline is an indication of our weakness, not our strength. If we refuse to practice, it is not God's grace that fails when a crisis comes, but our own nature. When the crisis comes, we ask God to help us, but he cannot if we have not made our nature our ally. The practicing is ours to do, not God's. God regenerates us and puts us in contact with all his divine resources, but he cannot make us walk according to his will. When we obey the Spirit and practice through our physical life all that God has put in our hearts, when a crisis comes, we will find we have not only God's grace to stand by us, but our own nature also. The crisis passes without disaster, and our soul, instead of being devastated, can actually acquire a stronger attitude toward God.

Remember that he has given us his Spirit, a helper in our training. We become like the boxer in the ring who constantly hears the words from the trainer in his corner. The Holy Spirit gives us instruction vital to our successful growth and cautions us when we are heading for trouble. Isn't it great to know that we have God in our corner all the way?

"Occasions make not a man fail, but they show what the man is." Thomas à Kempis.

NOT FOR PENANCE OR MERIT

We must be very careful here to recognize discipline for what it is, as well as for what it is not. Discipline is not practiced to gain merit with God or man. Our works cannot bring God any closer than he is already. As believers, our confessed sins have been forgiven already and do not have to be defined or refined by self-punishment. Each discipline should be practiced with a focus on God's goodness and provision. For instance, in the discipline of fasting, each time our bodies want food, we train our thoughts on God's goodness to us, or remember a particular Scripture, God's holy Word, as food for our spirits. Fasting trains our minds on a Father who provides our every need.

SUBMISSION

These disciplines constitute the indirect, yet vitally necessary submission of our body and its members to righteousness. How? I submit my tongue as an instrument of righteousness when I *make* it bless them that curse me and pray for them who persecute me, even though it automatically tends to strike and wound those who have wounded me. I submit my legs to God as instruments of righteousness when I engage them in physical labor as service, perhaps carrying a burden the second mile for someone whom I would rather let my legs kick. I submit my body to righteousness when I do my good deeds without letting them be known, though my whole frame cries out to strut and crow. And when I do, I offer up my body as the place of God's action. I prepare myself for God's action in me just as Abraham prepared the sacrifice in Genesis 15 and would have no fire touch it but what God himself sent. We do the righteous deed *because* of our redemption, not *for* our redemption. Our eyes are fixed upon God who is our life and who sets us free from the bondage to all that is less than himself, including the bondage of righteous deeds.

25. Can our deeds/works bring us closer to God?

_____

_____

_____

26. Are our practices of discipline penance for bad things we've done? Explain.

_____

_____

_____

27. True or False: The harder I work for God the more he will love me. Explain.

_____

_____

_____

Do not work for food that spoils, but for food that endures to eternal life, which the Son of Man will give you. On him God the Father has placed his seal of approval. 28 Then they asked him, "What must we do to do the works God requires?" 29 Jesus answered, "The work of God is this: to believe in the one he has sent." (John 6:27–29)

Let's look at the examples of disciplines Jesus demonstrated throughout his life.

Often, when Jesus practiced a discipline, he went to a private place. He did not announce what he was about to do or talk about it in public. His actions were private and personal. Obviously, some of the disciplines mentioned below were practiced in a public setting for God's glory, so that the people who saw his actions could know more fully God's love for them. Vain glory—personal glory—is not the goal for these disciplines; rather, it is to put forth God's active participation in our lives and to know him more fully.

28. Should you look for praise from men each time you do a good deed?

_____

_____

_____

But when you give to the needy, do not let your left hand know what your right hand is doing, 4 so that your giving may be in secret. Then your Father, who sees what is done in secret, will reward you. (Matthew 6:3–4)

FASTING

In the beginning of Jesus' ministry, after he had made himself known to John the Baptist, he went into the desert where he fasted for forty days. He knew he was going to be doing battle with Satan there so he trained his mind on the Scriptures, and with it rebuffed each temptation brought by the devil.

Satan tempted him to break his fast, to prove his deity by jumping down from a high cliff so that the angels would catch him, and to worship Satan himself with a bribe of kingship over an earthly territory. Each time Jesus quoted Scripture and referred to the one true God. He was able to focus all his attention on his God-given strength to vanquish the tempter. He was successful because he was disciplined. He knew the Scriptures and God's power ahead of time, before the battle. The *discipline* was in the learning and practice, ahead of the battle. No prizefighter goes into a fight without months of intense practice. So like Jesus, yes, even Jesus, we must practice self-discipline.

PRAYER

When Jesus prayed, he went to a private place. Even in the Garden of Gethsemane he left his disciples and went farther into the garden where he could be alone with his Father. There he prayed earnestly for the strength to accept what lay ahead of him—death on a cross. He prepared for his death long before he was nailed to the cross. His strength was in knowing the will of his Father; that knowledge and understanding came long before the suffering. He was ready before the trial.

Christians should pray every day. You can pray anywhere, anytime—on your way to work or in a crowded room. God hears us no matter where we are. If you are new at this, remember that any prayer, if from the heart, is all that is required. You don't have to use flowery speech or scholarly terms. God sees us as his children and wants us to express how we feel, our hopes and our troubles. Whatever you ask for, ask in Jesus' name.

A mealtime prayer could be as simple as, "Father, I thank you for the food you have provided for today. May it bless my body, and may I do your will, in Jesus' name. Amen."

Scripture tells us that the prayers of a righteous man have great power. We also read that some men prayed long, wordy prayers in public just to get attention. God looks at our private hearts, not our public works and long speeches.

READING AND STUDYING

Reading and studying God's holy Word began for Jesus at an early age. Scripture tells us that Jesus surprised the teachers in the synagogue by what he knew as a young man of twelve years. Through that illustration, we know that he must have spent much time in study. We read that Jesus grew in wisdom and in stature and in favor with God and man. His entire God/man self was growing and learning and practicing as he lived on the earth.

The experience of knowing God does not begin when our mortal lives have ebbed and gone. It begins the moment we become a redeemed child of God. This is the beginning of life eternal. Here, practicing begins and continues till we see Jesus face to face and know him fully.

If you are a new Christian, begin by reading the gospel of John in the New Testament section of the Bible. There you will learn what it means to be a Christ follower. Once you finish the book of John, read the remainder of the New Testament. Take time to understand what you read. Obtain study helps from your local Bible bookstore that will give helpful comments. Check your church library for study guides that you can borrow. Ask your pastor for resource suggestions.

Read your Bible every day. Rereading and memorization of helpful verses increases their usefulness. We need to be able to remember God's Word so that we may use it as Jesus did against Satan in the encounter in the desert. Jesus quoted Old Testament Scripture often in his earthly ministry to make a point or correct false teaching.

Get a reader-friendly version of the Bible. The New International Version and the Living Bible are two examples that are easy to read. There are many versions in print and prices range from as little as five dollars up to hundreds of dollars. Look for one that has study helps and notes in the margins. These help you understand difficult verses. You may want to build a library of helpful sources such as a Bible dictionary; which helps with Bible terms and talks about the history of people and places mentioned in Scripture. A concordance gives reference sites for every word used in Scripture; it helps you locate verses quickly. A book of biblical maps includes places mentioned in Scripture and what certain territories looked like during that time period. A commentary expounds on each verse in the Bible and helps us understand difficult passages. There are short studies available on each book of the Bible; you will also find studies on Bible characters or topics such as love, loneliness, etc.

God wants us to come to him each day to talk with him and read his Word. Living the Christian life without reading God's Word is like baking a cake without a recipe. You can guess at what the ingredients are and hope all will go well, or you can know for sure by reading and following the instructions.

JOIN A CHURCH AND FIND A GOOD TEACHER

Find a church that teaches from the Bible and begin to learn from an experienced teacher. I attend a church where there are several good teachers with lots of experience. Don't be afraid to ask a teacher how long he or she has been teaching. They will be glad you are careful in your selection. Ask a teacher how he or she became a teacher. Ask a teacher how they became a Christian. Good teachers have prayed about their position, seeking God's guidance for the job. Look for someone who is more mature in the faith. Ask how long they have been a Christian. (I want to be careful here to point out that no one will have all the answers to every question regarding Scripture. Each believer is in the maturation process. None of us has arrived at total Christian maturity. It is a process that is life long.)

SILENCE AND SOLITUDE

Jesus often sought a quiet place for rest, thought, and prayer.

Silence and solitude can be a practiced discipline. Far too many useless words have cluttered our lives till we almost fear silence. Many people cannot sit in silence at all.

God says, ". . . be still and know that I am God." How are you at singling out God's voice above the din in your own life? Can you hear him if you are never still? Reserving that most precious time with your Father can bring about surprising enlightenment and help you to hear personalized communication from him. Even in our prayer time we need to take time to be quiet and let God reveal his Word for us for that moment. Practice carving out a quiet time with God alone. That includes taking the phone off the hook, for that time belongs to God.

WORSHIP

Often, throughout Jesus' ministry, he could be found in the synagogue studying and worshiping his Father.

Worship should occur in private and with others. This is a wonderful discipline, where we can glorify God's awesome personality. Worship should be a part of every day with him. John 19:37–40 tells us that if we don't glorify and worship God the very rocks will cry out in praise to him. This activity affirms who our loving Father is and fills our hearts with joy. It is good to give thanks to God and bless his holy name. The Bible is full of the wonderful attributes and names of God: Savior, Lord, The Rock, A Firm Foundation, Creator, Healer, Everlasting Father, Prince of Peace. He has given his all for us and we should praise him for it. God inhabits the praise of his people. Singing is part of the worship experience. We may sing a song about God or one that addresses him personally. Praising him in any form is appropriate worship.

> Let them praise his name with dancing and make music to him with tambourine and harp. (Psalm 149–3)

CELEBRATION

Be a Christian who celebrates what God is doing in your life. Did you get a raise? Celebrate God's provision for you and your family. Have you had a specific answer to prayer? Celebrate God's goodness and his love. God wants us to be happy and to dance and sing and celebrate. God enjoys a good *yippee* or a heart-felt *wahoo*!

A cheerful look brings joy to the heart, and good news gives health to the bones. (Proverbs 15:30)

Let Israel [God's people] rejoice in their Maker; let the people of Zion be glad in their King. 3 Let them praise his name with dancing and make music to him with tambourine and harp. 4 For the Lord takes delight in his people; he crowns the humble with salvation. 5 Let the saints rejoice in this honor and sing for joy on their beds. (Psalm 149:2–5)

FELLOWSHIP

Fellowship for the believer is very important. That is the time we can share our experiences with others, and can find refreshing wells of water in fellowship with other believers. Each member of the body of Christ is given special talents and gifts, which are exercised with the rest of the body. There the student finds a teacher, the grieving find soothing hearts, and the worker finds like minds and helping hands to share the load. A family bonding takes place as we worship, pray, and study corporately. Fellowship with other believers broadens our community and stimulates us to use our God-given gifts. In giving and receiving, we take an active part in the whole body of Christ. In the New Testament churches, started by apostles like Paul, small cell churches met in homes, sharing everything. They ate together and even sold what they had to share the profits with their brothers and sisters in Christ.

And let us consider how we may spur one another on toward love and good deeds. 25 Let us not give up meeting together, as some are in the habit of doing, but let us encourage one another—and all the more as you see the Day approaching (which is your final day on this earth). (Hebrews 10:24–25)

You will be blessed greatly when you fellowship with and get to know your Christian family.

GIVING

The Bible says we are to give a tenth of our income to God. If we are faithful, he will bless us and teach us that he will multiply money given to him for his kingdom. Giving should be done from the heart in obedience. Giving begrudgingly will not bless you.

Time is a most valuable commodity—often harder to give than money. God richly blesses us when we give our time and talents to his work. Worship through tithes and offerings is an expression of our thankfulness to God for all that he gives us so freely.

A WORD ABOUT SERVICE AND GIVING

Be careful not to do your acts of righteousness before men, to be seen by them. If you do, you will have no reward from your Father in heaven. 2 So when you give to the needy, do not announce it with trumpets, as the hypocrites do in the syna-gogues and on the streets, to be honored by men. I tell you the truth. They have received their reward in full. 3 But when you give to the needy, do not let your left hand know what your right hand is doing, (in other words keep the deed to yourself alone) 4 so that your giving may be in secret. Then your Father, who sees what is done in secret, will reward you. (Matthew 6:1–4)

When you watch your plants grow in the gar-den, remember that they give and take in their growth. They give off oxygen and take in light, food, and water. Like the plant, it is essential for active Christians to give as well as receive. As you receive, do so with a thankful heart, allowing others to give to you; a practice in humility. It blesses the giver when we receive gratefully as well as gracefully.

SERVICE

Jesus demonstrated the discipline of service every-where he went. Though some thought of him in kingly terms, he set an example of a servant instead. Humility and service went hand in hand. He gave of himself without a sense of pride and set an ex-ample for others to follow.

A servant's heart looks for nothing in return, not even praise. As we grow in our walk with the Lord, we will begin finding ways to serve others. Remember that God does not look at the servant's works but at the servant's heart. Because of God's gift of salvation, our hearts overflow into service to others. Please allow others to give to you as well. Allow them the blessings of giving too.

CONFESSION

The old phrase, *confession is good for the soul*, is true. We might be less than honest about ourselves with others, but we must be forthright with God. He knows our every thought and deed anyway. Confessing our sins to God acknowledges our humanness and reminds us of God's goodness and desire to forgive. Confessing our sins brings them into focus for ourselves so that we might make every effort, with God's help, to resist them in the future. You and God are in this together. In your prayer time, confess your sins and ask God for forgiveness. God is faithful to forgive our sins even if we have to ask forgiveness of that same sin more than once. We are all human and from time to time find that a particular sin may recur in our lives more often. When Peter asked Jesus, "How many times shall I forgive my fellow man?" Jesus replied, "Seventy times seven." In biblical terms, that meant every time.

TRAINING YOUR HEART AND MIND

Finally, brothers, whatever is true, whatever is noble, whatever is right, whatever is pure, whatever is lovely, whatever is admirable—if anything is excellent or praiseworthy-think about such things. 9 Whatever you have learned or received or heard from me, or seen in me—put it into practice. And the God of peace will be with you. (Philippians 4:8–9)

Train your mind to think about praiseworthy things.

What did you watch on television yesterday, or look for on the Web? Was it good for your mind, body, and spirit? Would you be ashamed if someone were to find you looking at or listening to what you watched and listened to yesterday?

Pray and ask God to help you find enjoyable and spiritually edifying programs. It doesn't mean you have to listen to gospel music twenty-four hours a day. Just be aware of the content of what you see and hear.

Do a heart check by asking yourself . . .

- Is this good for my spirit?
- Is this bad for my spirit?

Some of us may be so calloused to what we watch that we aren't even conscious of its damaging influence on us.

OVER ALL YOU DO, POUR ON LOVE?

Love—the whole world recognizes it—yet if you asked twenty different people to define it, you would get at least as many different responses. God's love and the world's love are very different. The world's love is demonstrated in various ways: kisses and hugs, hearts and flowers, sweet ideas of men and women skipping through the daisies hand in hand together. Forever? Not very often. Why? Because mankind is vain and insists that his love is returned, and when that does not happen, he withdraws his love. Love, as mankind defines it, has an end, and often what takes its place is just the opposite, hate. Mankind despises those who hurt him, and the love is gone, squelched like a water-drenched fire. This poetic version of love is far from the love of God and in his Word we find examples of his love for us and the love we are to demonstrate toward others.

First, let's see where God ranks love in his plan for us.

> Hearing that Jesus had silenced the Sadducees, the Pharisees got together. 35 One of them, an expert in the law, tested him with this question: 36 "Teacher, which is the greatest commandment in the Law?" 37 Jesus replied, "Love the Lord your God with all your heart and with all your soul and with all your mind. 38 This is the first and greatest commandment. 39 And the second is like it: Love your neighbor as yourself. 40 All the Law and the Prophets hang on these two commandments." (Matthew 22:34–40)

In this Scripture Jesus says very plainly that love of others is second only to the love we give to God. Let me say that again, "Second only to our love for God." We can conclude then that great importance is placed on our love for others. What does this love look like? We can find the answer in Romans 12:2: "Do not conform any longer to the pattern of this world, but be transformed by the renewing of your mind." Paul, the writer of Romans, tells us that we are not to think like the world thinks, but to begin to see the world as God sees it, and as Jesus demonstrated in his life and ministry.

> Love must be sincere. Hate what is evil; cling to what is good. [Notice that this does not say, hate *who* is evil, but hate what is evil. This next portion spells out clearly how we are to love one another.]

10 Be devoted to one another in brotherly love. Honor one another above yourselves. 11 Never be lacking in zeal [enthusiasm], but keep your spiritual fervor, serving the Lord. 12 Be joyful in hope, patient in affliction, faithful in prayer. 13 Share with God's people who are in need. Practice hospitality. 14 Bless those who persecute you; bless and do not curse. 15 Rejoice with those who rejoice; and mourn with those who mourn. 16 Live in harmony with one another. Do not be proud, but be willing to associate with people of low position. Do not be conceited. 17 Do not repay anyone evil for evil. Be careful to do what is right in the eyes of everybody. 18 If it is possible, as far as it depends on you, live at peace with everyone. 19 Do not take revenge, my friends, but leave room for God's wrath, for it is written; "It is mine to avenge. I will repay," says the Lord. 20 On the contrary: "If your enemy is hungry, feed him; if he is thirsty, give him something to drink. In doing this, you will heap burning coals on his head." [Melt him into repentance and friendship.] 21 Do not overcome by evil, but overcome evil with good. (Romans 12:9–21)

Be imitators of God, therefore, as dearly loved children 2 and live a life of love, just as Christ loved us and gave himself up for us as a fragrant offering and sacrifice to God. (Ephesians 5:1–2)

And now I will show you the most excellent way. If I speak in the tongues of men and of angels, but have no love, I am only a resounding gong or a clanging cymbal. 2 If I have the gift of prophecy and can fathom all mysteries and all knowledge, and if I have a faith that can move mountains, but have not love, I am nothing. 3 If I give all I possess to the poor and surrender my body to the flames, but have not love, I gain nothing. 4 Love is patient, love is kind, It does not envy, it does not boast, it is not proud. 5 It is not rude, it is not self-seeking, it is not easily angered, it keeps no record of wrongs. 6 Love does not delight in evil but rejoices with the truth. 7 It always protects, always trusts, always hopes, always perseveres. 8 Love never fails. But where there are prophecies, they will cease; where there are tongues, they will be stilled; where there is knowledge, it will pass away. 9 For we know in part and we prophesy in part, 10 but when perfection comes, the imperfect disappears. 11 When I was a child, I talked like a child, I thought like a child, I reasoned like a child. When I became a man, I put childish ways behind me. 12 Now we see but a poor reflection as in a mirror; then I shall know fully, even as I am fully known. 13 And now these three remain: faith, hope and love. But the greatest of these is love. (1 Corinthians 13:1–13)

The Bible is full of demonstrations of love. Jesus was best at showing it. He demonstrated, through his life here on earth, God's love for us. And, greatest of all, he showed man ultimate love by dying on the cross for our sins. In love he gave us new life and made us heirs, children of God. We can demonstrate our love for him by keeping his commands; by loving him first and our fellow man as we love ourselves.

29. On the lines below, list all the things love is not.

_____

_____

_____

30. Now list the things that love is.

_____

_____

_____

31. We can attain many worthy attributes and still not have love; 1 Corinthians 13 tells us what these are. List them below.

_____

_____

_____

32. On what parts of your life do you need to
    pour on love?

_____

_____

_____

Stop and pray right now. Ask God to fill you
with his love and teach you how to love those in
your life who may be difficult to love. Ask God to
help you demonstrate his love to everyone. God will
be faithful to answer if we are faithful to ask. Keep a
record of your progress.

ON A PERSONAL NOTE

When I know I am going to be spending time with
someone I find hard to love, I begin to pray far in
advance of that meeting. I also ask my friends to
pray for me and for the person I am going to meet.
God works on us and in us if we submit to his leadership and power.

> But he said to me, "My grace is sufficient for you,
> for my power is made perfect in weakness." There-
> fore I will boast all the more gladly about my weak-
> nesses, so that Christ's power may rest on me. 10
> That is why, for Christ's sake, I delight in weak-
> nesses, in insults, in hardships, in persecutions,

in difficulties. For when I am weak, then I am strong. (2 Corinthians 12:9–10)

AN EXAMPLE OF LEADERSHIP IN THE EARLY CHURCH

In the book of Titus we are given the characteristics that an elder (church leader) should demonstrate. In Titus 1:6–9 Paul writes:

> An elder must be blameless, the husband of but one wife, a man whose children believe and are not open to the charge of being wild and disobedient. 7 Since an overseer is entrusted with God's work, he must be blameless—not overbearing, not quick-tempered, not given to drunkenness, not violent, not pursuing dishonest gain. 8 Rather he must be hospitable, one who loves what is good, who is self-controlled, upright, holy and disciplined. 9 He must hold firmly to the trustworthy message as it has been taught, so that he can encourage others by sound doctrine and refute those who oppose it.

If you are doing this study in a group, discuss why these characteristics are important for leadership.

WHAT DOES WATER REALLY DO FOR PLANTS?

We have already talked a little about the necessity of water for growing things. Now let's look at what water really does for plants. Water taken up by the roots of a plant moves nutrients up through the stem of the plant. The plant respires the water out through its leaves, which causes more water to be drawn up through the stem. Photosynthesis* through the leaves provides food for the plant to use. Water moves these nutrients back down the plant stems and the plant thrives.

THE EVERLASTING WATER

Christ is the water that flows through us and provides through the Holy Spirit nutrients/food for our spirit and our well being.

33. What are some problems that can occur when we exclude water/living water from plants or ourselves?

_____

_____

_____

I delight greatly in the Lord; my soul rejoices in my God. For he has clothed me with garments of salvation and arrayed me in a robe of righteousness, as a bridegroom adorns his head like a priest, and as a bride adorns herself with her jewels. 11 For as the earth brings forth its shoots, and as a garden causes what is sewn in it to spring up, so the Lord God will cause righteousness and praise to spring up before all the nations. (Isaiah 61:10–11)

What is righteousness? Righteousness is being right with God. Why should we be right with God? *The Holman Bible Dictionary* states it as follows: The one who in faith gives oneself to the doing of God's will is righteous, doing righteousness and reckoned righteous by God (James 2:23).

34. What does it mean to be arrayed in robes of righteousness?

_____

_____

_____

35. Compare what you thought about becoming righteous as a nonbeliever with what you know now.

_____

_____

_____

We can say God is doing a work in and through us by the living water—Jesus Christ.

Take a break, be still, and ask God to reveal his work in you. What he is doing now? What is he asking you to begin doing? If you can, share this with others. God is so diverse; you may be amazed at what others will say. Remember his ways are not our ways. Scripture tells us that God has already prepared the way for us to do his will. How awesome is that?

> But because of his great love for us, God, who is rich in mercy, 5 made us alive with Christ even when we were dead in transgressions—it is by grace you have been saved. 6 And God raised us up with Christ and seated us with him in the heavenly realms in Christ Jesus, 7 in order that in the coming ages he might show the incomparable riches of his grace, expressed in his kindness to us in Christ Jesus. 8 For it is by grace you have been saved, through faith—and this not from yourselves, it is the gift of God—9 not by works, so that no one can boast. 10 For we are God's workmanship, created in Christ Jesus to do good works, which God prepared in advance for us to do. (Ephesians 2:4–10)

Grace: undeserved acceptance and love received from another, especially the characteristic attitude of God in providing salvation for sinners *(Holman Bible Dictionary)*.

Mercy: A personal characteristic of care for the needs of others *(Holman Bible Dictionary)*.

36. God has raised us to what position? What do you think this means?

_____

_____

_____

37. What will God show us in the coming ages?

_____

_____

_____

38. What is the gift of God?

_____

_____

_____

39. a. Can we earn our salvation? Explain.

_____

_____

_____

b. How does this make us all equal in God's sight?

_____

_____

_____

FIRST SIGNS OF LIFE

Our plant has begun to come up through the soil and has produced a root system. Tiny, round leaves pop out on our baby plant. These leaves nourish the new plant and give it energy to grow more. These little leaves are called cotyledons*. In a week or two the plant will put out different kinds of leaves: bigger, broader leaves that will spread out and catch the sunlight and will exchange moisture for the plant. These are life-sustaining necessities for the plant.

New believers are very tender as well. They have only begun to establish their roots in God's Word and will need much gentle care. If you are a new believer, seek after the essentials for growth, the *light* of the world, our Lord and Savior; *food*, God's holy

Word and the everlasting, thirst-quenching *water*, Jesus Christ.

A seed given light, food and water will begin to grow. Remember, savor each new change, and be patient, as great things will take time! Quite honestly, we should continue to grow and learn for an entire lifetime, applying all we have learned. The application of God's Word is wisdom.

We have learned about the wonderful beginning of a walk with the Lord and the start of our delicate little zinnia plant. (Those planting for an indoor garden may want to plant thyme, basil, or parsley, since their demand for direct sun is less.)

What comes next is just as important for the success of a believer/plant.

THIN OUT! HARDEN OFF! TRANSPLANT!

Garden experts say the next few steps are the hardest to do. We have planted these little seeds and watched in awe as they came up through the ground. They're so tiny and tender.

When a plant has come through the ground and has its little feeder leaves (cotyledon*) we must treat it like a little baby. But inevitably, we want that little baby to be a healthy adult plant. This means we are going to watch for the next few pairs of leaves to form. They will look like the leaves of the adult plant. When we see these leaves, it's time to treat our plant a little differently. For our baby to survive, we must now thin out what is weak and reduce the competing seedlings so that strong seedlings will grow successfully.

What Should I Thin Out, as a Christian?

God wants us to remove anything that is in competition with him in our lives. Below are two scriptural examples of competition. In Matthew 4:10, Jesus said to Peter, "Away from me, Satan! For it is written: Worship the Lord your God, and serve him only." And again in Luke 16:13, Jesus said, "No servant can serve two masters. Either he will hate the one and love the other, or he will be devoted to the one and despise the other. You cannot serve both God and money."

40. Everyone needs money to live. How can money come between us and God?

_____

_____

_____

41. How can wealth be used by God?

_____

_____

_____

Therefore, get rid of all moral filth and the evil that is so prevalent and humbly accept the word planted in you, which can save you. (James 1:21)

In Exodus, Moses met with God on a mountain. There, God gave the people ten basic laws to follow. First on the list was: You shall have no other gods before me. God did not mince words here at all. He stated quite clearly that he alone was God and that man should not put any other god ahead of him.

Ancient peoples worshiped many gods. Each god was man-made; the demands and philosophies were thought up by men. Today we worship other gods too; our gods today can be great wealth, a large home, an expensive car, world-wide fame, or even our children. None of these examples is sinful in itself, but each can become so if we spend all our time, money, and thought on acquiring them. God wants to be first in our lives. If we put him first, he will bless us with good things and we will learn what he has intended for us, which is far better than anything we might imagine. He asks us to put our faith in him.

42. Who or what is first in your life today?

_____

_____

_____

43. How should we serve God?

_____

_____

_____

Therefore each of you must put off falsehood and speak truthfully to his neighbor, for we are all members of one body. 26 In your anger do not sin: Do not let the sun go down while you are still angry, 27 and do not give the devil a foothold. 28 He who has been stealing must steal no longer, but must work, doing something useful with his own hands, that he may have something to share with those in need. 29 Do not let any unwholesome talk come out of your mouths, but only what is helpful for building others up according to their needs, that it may benefit those who listen. 30 And do not grieve the Holy Spirit of God, with whom you were sealed for the day of redemption. 31 Get rid of all bitterness, rage and anger, brawling and slander, along with every form of malice. 32 Be kind and compassionate to one another, forgiving each other, just as in Christ, God forgave you. (Ephesians 4:25–32)

44. What do these verses tell us must be eliminated and thinned out?

_____

_____

_____

45. What in your life is competing with your godly growth?

_____

_____

_____

WHAT DOES THE BIBLE SAY ABOUT:

Lying?

Nowhere in the entire Bible can we find a lie that is described as little or white. In the book of Exodus, Abraham lied, saying his wife Sarah was his sister. He was found out both times.

There are six things the Lord hates, seven that are detestable to him: 17 Haughty eyes, a lying tongue, hands that shed innocent blood, 18 a heart that devises wicked schemes, feet that are quick to rush into evil, 19 a false witness who pours out lies and a man who stirs up dissension among brothers. (Proverbs 6:16–19)

Anger?

Is anger a sin? Psalm 4:4 says: "In your anger do not sin. Jesus' anger became apparent when he saw that the courts of the temple in Jerusalem were filled with money changers instead of worshipers. He turned over their tables and said they had made the courts a den of robbers." Was his anger sinful? No.

Sinful anger causes us to do evil to ourselves and others and to abandon our self-control; one of the many fruits of the spirit. James 1:19; "My dear brothers, take note of this: Everyone should be quick to listen, slow to speak and slow to become angry."

If you find that you are too often angry, you should ask yourself why. What makes me angry? Many times there is a pattern to frequent anger. Seek help from a professional if you feel angry often. You can manage your anger by asking God to help.

Stealing?

Stealing is prohibited in Exodus 20:15, and is listed as one of the Ten Commandments given by God to Moses for the people of Israel. It is against God's law and man's law today.

Unwholesome Talk?

Above, Ephesians 4:29 explains that talking should be for the edification of other believers. In Titus 1:10, Paul warns against teaching for dishonest gain, and name calling. Paul tells believers to rebuke such people sharply so that they will be sound in their faith.

> If anyone considers himself religious and yet does not keep a tight rein on his tongue, he deceives himself and his religion is worthless. (James 1:26)

In chapter 3:3–8 James gives a scorching description of the unruly tongue.

> When we put bits into the mouths of horses to make them obey us, we can turn the whole animal. 4 Or take ships as an example. Although they are so large and are driven by strong winds, they are steered by a very small rudder wherever the pilot wants to go. 5 Likewise, the tongue is a small part of the body, but it makes great boasts. Consider what a great forest is set on fire by a small spark. 6 The tongue also is a fire, a world of evil

among the parts of the body. It corrupts the whole person, sets the whole course of his life on fire, and is itself set on fire by hell. 7 All kinds of animals, birds, reptiles and creatures of the sea are being tamed and have been tamed by man, 8 but no man can tame the tongue. It is a restless evil, full of deadly poison.

46. How is the tongue like a small spark?

_____

_____

_____

47. How can the tongue be full of deadly poison? Give some examples.

_____

_____

_____

You shall not misuse the name of the Lord your God, for the Lord will not hold anyone guiltless who misuses his name. (Exodus 20:7)

This passage tells us to guard our tongues against abusive swearing in the Lord's name or cursing others with his name.

With the tongue we praise our Lord and Father, and with it we curse men, who have been made in God's likeness. 10 Out of the same mouth come praise and cursing. My brothers, this should not be. (James 3:9–10)

Again you have heard that it was said to the people long ago, 'Do not break your oath, but keep the oaths you have made to the Lord.' 34 But I tell you, Do not swear at all: either by heaven, for it is God's throne; 35 or by the earth, for it is his footstool; or by Jerusalem, for it is the city of the Great King. 36 And do not swear by your head, for you cannot make even one hair white or black. 37 Simply let your "yes" be "yes" and your "no" be "no"; anything beyond this comes from the evil one. (Matthew 5:33–37)

Here we see that we are to be trustworthy and mean what we say. When we are asked to do something and agree to do it, we must be faithful to our answer. Otherwise, our word begins to mean nothing to those who depend on our true answer. A promise is a promise; so don't ever promise anything to anyone unless you mean to back it up with action. This especially includes your children. They must see that you mean what you say, otherwise they will begin to be frustrated by meaningless promises. The value of a promise is in keeping the promise after all. Mean what you say and say what you mean.

WHAT DOES THE BIBLE SAY ABOUT GRIEVING THE HOLY SPIRIT?

The dictionary says: grieve is a verb which means to suffer grief, to cause great distress to. The Holy Spirit has been sent to each believer. He dwells within each of us and is perfect. Those who grieve the Holy Spirit are grieving God. Our disobedience of any God-given instruction grieves the Holy Spirit. Any sin is unacceptable to God, thus his redemptive plan is for a sinful people.

Bitterness?

> If you harbor bitter envy and selfish ambition in your hearts, do not boast about it or deny the truth. This does not come from heaven but is earthly, unspiritual and of the devil. (James 3:14)

Bitter is a noun which means marked by cynicism and rancor; exhibiting intense animosity.

Rage?

In Acts 4:23–27 Peter and John pray with their people and quote from Psalm 2. They link rage and conspiracy together. Rage begets conspiracy and is described as violent anger accompanied with furious words, gestures, or agitation; an anger excited to fury.

Brawling?

As a noun, brawl means a rough or noisy fight or quarrel. As a verb—to take part in a brawl.

Women watch out! Proverbs 21:9 says it is better to live on a corner of the roof than to share a house with a brawling woman. Even though women are used for this example, it does not exempt men. No spirit can be at peace when quarreling occurs. Discover its cause and strive to make peace with your opponent. Do not be so quick to blame another, for it takes two to quarrel. Ask God to help you find a solution.

> Flee the evil desires of youth, and pursue righteousness, faith, love and peace, along with those who call on the Lord out of a pure heart. 23 Don't have anything to do with foolish and stupid arguments, because you know they produce quarrels. 24 And the Lord's servant must not quarrel, instead, he must be kind to everyone, able to teach, not resentful. 25 Those who oppose him he must *gently* instruct, in the hope that God will grant them repentance leading them to a knowledge of the truth, 26 and that they will come to their senses and escape from the trap of the devil, who has taken them captive to do his will. (2 Timothy 2:22–26)

Malice?

Malice is the disposition to injure others for mere personal gratification, or from a spirit of revenge, spite; ill-will.

> At one time we too were foolish, disobedient, deceived, and enslaved by all kinds of passions and pleasures. We lived in malice and envy, being hated and hating one another. 4 But when the kindness and love of God our Savior appeared, 5 he saved us, not because of righteous things we had done, but because of his mercy. He saved us through the washing of rebirth and renewal by the Holy Spirit. (Titus 3:3–5)

Forgiveness?

Jesus taught in the Lord's Prayer that we will be forgiven in the same measure as we forgive others. That is plain and simple. We are not responsible for what another may harbor in his or her heart, only what we harbor in our own. God holds each of us accountable for our own heart's condition.

ACTIVITY # 4

Thinning Out

In our real garden we are ready to thin out our crop of small seedlings. We want to select only the strongest and eliminate competition. In each seed cell, leave just one little plant. Cut out extras and undesirables at ground level with small scissors, allowing only our choice plants to use the nutrient supply available in the soil. Eliminating competition and crowding increases air flow and light to the plant. Now our little seedlings can get stronger and begin to develop into healthy, mature plants.

TIME OUT!

Take time right now. Be very quiet and ask your loving God to show you what may be competing with him. This may or may not be something you want to share with others, but write it down in a place where you will see it. Remember to pray and ask God to help you begin work in this area. Many things that compete have very strong roots. Some teeth gritting and tugging may be necessary.

This may be a good time to try the discipline of silence. Spend a few hours without talking and listen to what God has to say to you. Make this a special time away from phones and other distractions.

THE DANDELION

Have you ever looked at your garden in the early spring and seen many, little, tiny plants? It's hard to tell what is a weed and what is a good plant. I've always marveled at the rapid growth of some weeds. The dandelion, for example, can become large very quickly. Have you ever tried to pull out a dandelion? "It's a dandy, lion-sized weed."

In our lives, small, innocent habits can grow into big problems if we don't eliminate them early. If we do not, we may end up with a deep-rooted, dandelion-sized problem.

In Ephesians 4:25–32 we learned some of the things we must get rid of, which we have already listed.

48. From this passage list the good things we should strive for.

_____

_____

_____

ACTIVITY # 5

Hardening Off

Once we have established the choice plants, we
now need to introduce these little sprouts to some
significant sun and heat. This is what gardeners
refer to as hardening off.* For the plant to survive in the great outdoors, it must become accli-
mated to the real world. The wind must buffet it
about, to get the stem to stand sturdy and straight.
The sun must shine on it for real. It must get used
to the heat. Each day our little plants should be
given increasingly longer periods of wind and sun.
Proper exposure to the elements helps plants grow
and mature. Begin by placing your plants outside
for an hour or two in the morning; afterward,
bring the plants back inside. Every day, increase
the time outside by a few minutes. Hardening off
takes about seven to ten days. You can build a

cold frame* for this purpose. Putting your plants in a cold frame outside eliminates moving plants back inside each day.

As Christians we do not want to become hardened as the world defines it, but rather, strong through trusting God's power and faithfulness through the trials of life.

TRIALS MAKE US STRONG

James writes in 1:2–4:

> Consider it pure joy, my brothers, whenever you face trials of many kinds, 3 because you know that the testing of your faith develops perseverance. 4 Perseverance must finish its work so that you may be mature and complete, not lacking anything.

At first, this may seem a very harsh statement. But when we look a little closer we find that James is talking about the joy as the result of a trial, not in the trial itself.

Christians are exposed to situations that make us strong and sturdy. Below we read about winds that blow, streams that rise, and rains that fall. To what situations in life can we compare these metaphors?

Therefore everyone who hears these words of mine and puts them into practice is like a wise man who built his house on the rock. 25 The rain came down, the stream rose, and the winds blew and beat against that house; yet it did not fall, because it had its foundation on the rock. 26 But every one who hears these words of mine and does not put them into practice is like a foolish man who built his house on sand. 27 The rain came down, the streams rose, and the winds blew and beat against that house, and it fell with a great crash. (Matthew 7:24–27)

In 1 Corinthians 10:4, Paul refers to Jesus as the rock. He is the foundation of our faith, the rock of our salvation.

Unlike a rock that stands firm, sand shifts with the tide and is blown by the wind. Sand moves and changes. Jesus is the same forever and we can be sure that he will remain where he can be found by each of us, located in us by the indwelling of the Holy Spirit.

49. Write some of the difficult events in your life that have made you stronger.

_____

_____

_____

50. How are you building a life (house) on the rock?

_____

_____

_____

51. What do you think causes people to build their lives (houses) on the sand?

_____

_____

_____

In Psalm 1 we read:

1 Blessed is the man who does not walk in the counsel of the wicked or stand in the way of sinners or sit in the seat of mockers. 2 But his delight is in the law of the Lord, and on his law he meditates day and night. 3 He is like a tree planted by streams of water, which yields its fruit in season and whose leaf does not wither. Whatever he does prospers. 4 Not so the wicked! They are like chaff that the wind blows away. 5 Therefore the wicked will not stand in the judgment, nor sinners in the assembly of the righteous. 6 For the Lord watches

over the way of the righteous, but the way of the wicked will perish.

52. Describe the differences between the blessed and the wicked.

_____

_____

_____

Centuries ago, when farmers raised grain in their fields they used a technique called winnowing to separate the chaff from the grain. They pitched the grain into the air, and the useless chaff or husks were blown away by the wind. The heavier grain fell back to the floor. The grain was then collected and used.

53. How are the wicked like chaff?

_____

_____

_____

God in his wisdom, power and love has created all things.

He knew you before you were born and knit you together in your mother's womb. (Psalm 139:13)

God cares about our successes and failures and provides for our every need. He knows what we need and want long before we do.

New Leaves and a Changed Look

As a plant grows from its infancy to new heights, the cotyledons are replaced by adult leaves. These leaves help identify the particular plant. But even these come from a tiny bud that matures with time. Leaves unfold to become a necessary part of the plant. Through these leaves the plant exercises its photosynthesis. Strip a plant of its leaves and the plant will die.

Why Not Just Stay a Baby in My New Faith?

What sensible parent ever wanted their child to stay a baby forever? Parents take great pride in their child's development. Growth is expected. Mothers and fathers become alarmed if their children do not develop at the proper pace.

As a mother of two, I adore my girls. I loved taking care of them when they were babies. I was thankful when they began to walk, talk, and tie their own shoes. They were becoming more mature because they remembered and practiced basic skills.

We grow in our faith in much the same way. By adding knowledge continually, and putting into practice what we learn, we grow to become more Christ-like. Ask yourself this question, "If I were arrested for being a Christian, would they find enough evidence to convict me?" What do you think your evidence is?

54. In what ways are you becoming more Christ-like today?

_____

_____

_____

FALSE DOCTRINES

Ephesians 4:14–15 reminds us of our calling and states that as we mature in our faith "we will no longer be infants, tossed back and forth by the waves, and blown here and there by every wind of teaching and by the cunning and craftiness of men in their deceitful scheming. Instead, speaking the truth in love, we will in all things *grow up* into him who is the Head, that is, Christ."

Paul, a convert to Christianity, and one of the first missionaries, sent letters to warn the new Christians in A.D. 50 about false teachers and man-made doctrines.

> I am astonished that you are so quickly deserting the one who called you by the grace of Christ and are turning to a different gospel 7 which is really no gospel at all. Evidently some people are throwing you into confusion and are trying to pervert the gospel of Christ. 8 But even if we or an angel from heaven should preach a gospel other than the one we preached to you, let him be eternally condemned! (Galatians 1:6–8)

> So then, just as you received Christ Jesus as Lord, continue to live in him, 7 rooted and built up in him, strengthened in the faith as you were taught, and overflowing with thankfulness. 9 See to it that no one takes you captive through hollow and deceptive philosophy, which depends on human tradition and the basic principles of this world rather than on Christ. (Colossians 2:6–9)

55. What will you do to be able to tell true doctrine from false?

_____

_____

_____

The world would tell us that there are many ways to God. John 10:1,7,9 Jesus said, "I tell you the truth, the man who does not enter the sheep pen by the gate, but climbs in by some other way, is a thief and a robber." 7 Therefore Jesus said again, "I tell you the truth, I am the gate for the sheep." 9 "I am the gate; whoever enters through me will be saved." John 11:25 "I am the resurrection and the life. He who believes in me will live, even though he dies."

Jesus paid the price for our sin with his shed blood. His death brought about our everlasting life; his resurrection demonstrated his power over death and the grave. Now we who believe in him are free to approach the throne and receive all that God intends for us.

First John teaches us how to test the spirits:

Dear friends, do not believe every spirit, but test the spirits to see whether they are from God, because many false prophets have gone out into the world. 2 this is how you can recognize the Spirit of God; Every spirit that acknowledges that Jesus Christ has come in the flesh is from God, 3 but every spirit that does not acknowledge Jesus, is not from God. This is the spirit of the antichrist, which you have heard is coming and even now is already in the world. 4 You, dear children, are from God and have overcome them, because the one who is in you is greater than the one who is in the world. 5 They are from the world and therefore speak from the viewpoint of the world, and the world listens to them. 6 We are from God, and whoever knows God listens to us; but whoever is not from God does not listen to us. This is how we recognize the spirit of truth and the spirit of falsehood. (4:1–6)

John told believers how to distinguish between godly and worldly spirits. The apostles who followed Christ taught these things to the first converts of Christianity; they are just as relevant to us today.

Timothy, a minister to one of the early churches, says in 1 Timothy 4:7–10:

Have nothing to do with godless myths and old wives' tales: rather, train yourself to be godly. 8 For physical training is of some value, but godliness has value for all things, holding promise for both the present life and the life to come. 9 This is a trustworthy saying that deserves full acceptance 10 (and for this we labor and strive), that we have put our hope in the living God, who is the Savior of all men, and especially of those who believe.

Take time now just to thank God for his mercy toward you and praise him. He delights in our praise, and thankfulness blesses our hearts.

ACTIVITY # 6

Transplanting Your New Plants

When you have hardened off your plants, you are ready to transplant your zinnias into the flowerbed you prepared earlier outside. If you are gardening on the patio, transplant you seedlings to bigger pots and set them in place on the patio. If you are gardening on the windowsill, move your herb seedlings to larger pots that fit your sill area.

If you are using this study at a time when planting outside is not possible, transplant your seedlings into separate, larger pots and place them under a grow light. Leave the light on twelve to fourteen hours a day, no more than eight inches from the tops of the plants. This will keep them from becoming spindly and toppling over. They can actually bud and bloom under the grow light.

With a Popsicle stick or spoon handle, nudge the plant from its container, maintaining its root system in the soil. Dig a hole equal to the size of the root and soil ball. Moisten the hole with water until a small puddle appears. Place your plant into the hole and cover the root ball with soil. Use a mixture of water-soluble fertilizer and water to moisten and fertilize the plant. Be sure to read instructions for mixing on the fertilizer container. Your new plant will need watching for a few days. Water, if needed, with a gentle spray. Do not use a harsh spray, as this can harm the plant or dislodge it from its new home. In time, the roots will develop and go deeper into the soil, establishing a hardy foundation for a thriving plant. You might even want to use a root stimulation solution. You can purchase this at your garden store. Read the instructions carefully and apply when you repot your seedlings. Watch how quickly your plant takes to its new home. It's easy to grow beautiful flowering plants, even in winter.

Your plant will begin to develop more and larger leaves. The stems will grow longer and longer and eventually produce fruiting flowers. (Flowers that will become the edible fruit or seed fruit of your plant.)

Have You Ever Been Transplanted?

Have you ever had to move to a new home far from familiar surroundings? My family made one major move. My husband Jim changed jobs. We had lived in Pennsylvania for fifteen years. My girls were in their teens and had lived in one place up to that point. We left behind a beautiful Christian fellowship, which we considered our extended family. In some ways that move was difficult. Our girls had to leave their childhood friends. Jim and I had to say good-bye to friends we had known for years.

As difficult as that move was, God had already prepared a place for us in our new community. We joined a new church that was full of loving people. We were automatically accepted and encouraged. Our girls were overwhelmed by the love of their new friends. That was a transplant made in heaven.

God's family circles the entire globe. If you find yourself uprooted, I urge you to find a group of fellow believers and become part of a new family in Christ. You'll be glad you did.

STUNTED GROWTH

Let's take a look at what stunted growth is and how it happens. Plants can become stunted when light, water, or food have decreased dramatically. The lack of any one of these plant stimuli can quickly change the health of our plant. Happily, an ill plant and a stunted Christian can be revived, if what is lacking is added. Those seeking God can digress in growth by the elimination of spiritual water, food, or the Son. But if we are careful to live in the light of God's love, respond to the leading of the Holy Spirit, meditate daily on God's Word and continue in prayer, we can be sure that growth will follow.

56. Let's review the three growth stimuli for healthy plants and Christians. Write them from memory here.

_____

_____

_____

As growing Christians we will experience difficult times; times when we feel like quitting. With both plant and man, time for maturation must be allowed and welcomed. God does not expect us to mature over night and we know that a plant cannot go from seed to fruit in the blink of an eye. We must learn that patience, one of the most difficult actions to apply, must be applied.

Sometimes waiting on God's timing is quite difficult, but he will sustain us through it. An active Christian will seek new growth for an entire lifetime. Did you know that some plants will actually quit growing if the temperature gets too cold or too hot? We, like plants, face the same problem. For example, when we distance ourselves from God, we become cold. This can stunt our growth. Distance occurs when we get too busy to read, pray, or practice the disciplines of our faith. Does God seem far away today? It is not because he has forgotten us, rather we have forgotten to make him the center of our lives. God is the same, yesterday, today, and forever. Stop and pray now and ask God to help you focus on your relationship with him.

Our obedience must come from our will, not our emotions. Exercise your faith in spite of your feelings. Persevere in spite of the hardships. In the verses below we can take comfort that God will be with us, and we need not worry.

> Look at the birds of the air; they do not sow or reap or store away in barns, and yet your heavenly Father feeds them. Are you not much more valuable than they? 27 Who of you by worrying can add a single hour to his life? . . . 34 Therefore do not worry about tomorrow, for tomorrow will worry about itself. Each day has enough trouble of its own. (Matthew 6:26–27, 34)

One very important thing to remember: every Christian has struggled and will struggle through the growth process. God is faithful to see us through each and every situation. The apostle Paul said, "We know what we ought to do, and do not do it." This can be a painful time as we struggle to give to God what we desperately want to keep and fix ourselves. Giving all things to God will grow our faith in him.

Learn what it is to trust God completely. Give him your burdens and faithfully seek him in prayer.

Be loving and patient with others. Each is on this journey and each is at a different place in the journey. Loving kindness and encouragement are soothing to a struggling soul.

Many Christians arrange to have an accountability partner. This partner should be a mature, trustworthy Christian, in whom you can confide. He or she can pray for specific personal problems you might have, and give advice and correction. Many pastors have accountability partners too. Recognizing their humanness, they seek guidance, correction, and prayer.

ENTERS THE STORM

Then we will no longer be infants, tossed back and forth by the waves, and blown here and there by every wind of teaching and by the cunning and craftiness of men in their deceitful scheming. 15 Instead, speaking the truth in love, we will in all things grow up into him who is the Head, that is, Christ. (Ephesians 4:14–15)

Notice that this Scripture doesn't say that there might be storms, or there may be winds. Instead, it includes them absolutely.

A plant can tolerate much from a storm. It can blow entirely flat and revive to perfect condition when the sun returns. Driving rain and strong wind can beat down a plant until it looks quite bedraggled. But a plant's resilience can bring it back to its former stature.

As Christians we can be sure that even though the storms are inevitable, God's grace is sufficient to bring us back to our former glory, with more wisdom and stamina than before. Wisdom comes from experience, and experience from stepping out in faith as God goes ahead and prepares the way in advance. We grow and learn to trust God more as time goes on.

Read Psalm 23 and note the times God has gone ahead of us to prepare the way. Note the times he moves to our side in danger and darkness.

The Lord is my shepherd, I shall not be in want. 2 He makes me lie down in green pastures, he leads me beside quiet waters, 3 He restores my soul. He guides me in paths of righteousness for his name's sake. 4 Even though I walk through the valley of the shadow of death, I will fear no evil, for you are with me; your rod and your staff, they comfort me. 5 You prepare a table before me in the presence of my enemies. You anoint my head with oil; my cup overflows. 6 Surely goodness and love will follow me all the days of my life, and I will dwell in the house of the Lord forever. (Psalm 23:1–6)

57. Make a list of the comforts the Lord offers his sheep. (Us)

_____

_____

_____

58. Can you think of a time in your life when adversity made you a stronger person? What did you learn from the experience?

_____

_____

_____

59. In what ways can you use these promises today? Write your plans for application, then come back later and write down your results.

Plans

_____

_____

_____

Results

_____

_____

60. On a separate sheet of paper, rewrite Psalm 23 in your own words, as if God were writing encouragement for you personally. Use your own name to personalize it.

Maybe you will want to start a journey journal where you can keep track of your growth, prayer requests, and answers to prayer. It's good to go back and read just how gracious and powerful God is in your life.

The prayers of a believer may be answered in several different ways. God may ask us to wait for an answer, or he may say yes or no to our requests. We must understand that God's ways are not ours and we must have faith in his wisdom. Sometimes the answers to our prayers come after our life here on earth is over. Pray believing, and leave the good timing to your heavenly father who loves us and gives good gifts in the proper season.

> Oh, the depth of the riches of the wisdom and knowledge of God! How unsearchable his judgments, and his paths beyond tracing out! 34 Who has known the mind of the Lord? Or who has been his counselor? 35 Who has ever given to God, that God should repay him? 36 For from him and through him and to him are all things. To him be the glory forever! Amen. (Romans 11:33–36)

In Job 38, God spells out his sovereignty, knowledge, and power. "Who is this that darkens my counsel with words without knowledge? Brace yourself like a man; I will question you, and you shall answer me. Where were you when I laid the earth's foundation? Tell me, if you understand. Who marked off its dimensions? Surely you know! Who stretched a measuring line across it? On what were its footings set, or who laid its cornerstone while the morning stars sang together and all the angels shouted for joy? Who shut up the sea behind doors when it burst forth from the womb, when I made the clouds its garment and wrapped it in thick darkness, when I fixed limits for it and set its doors and bars in place, when I said, 'This far you may come and no farther; here is where your proud waves halt?' Have you ever given orders to the morning, or shown the dawn its place, that it might take the earth by the edges and shake the wicked out of it?"

This powerful passage continues as God lists the multitude of things that only he can know. Read it in its entirety directly from your Bible and gain a greater understanding of who your God is.

BEARING FRUIT ·

By God's grace, in the power of the Spirit, man's whole life is transformed. These are the signs of that transformation. The apostle Paul identifies these fruits of the Spirit for us in Galatians 5:22–23: love, joy, peace, patience, kindness, goodness, faithfulness, gentleness and self-control.

> Let us not become weary in doing good [loving others], for at the proper time we will reap a harvest if we do not give up. (Galatians 6:9)

61. List each of the fruits of the Spirit here and beside each entry write the name of someone you know who demonstrates this particular characteristic.

_____

_____

_____

_____

_____

_____

_____

_____

_____

In Matthew 7:15–20 a fruitful tree is described for us.

15 Watch out for false prophets. They come to you in sheep's clothing, but inwardly they are ferocious wolves. 16 By their fruit you will recognize them. Do people pick grapes from thorn bushes, or figs from thistles? 17 Likewise every good tree bears good fruit, but a bad tree bears bad fruit. 18 A good tree cannot bear bad fruit, and a bad tree cannot bear good fruit. 19 Every tree that does not bear good fruit is cut down and thrown into the fire. 20 Thus, by their fruit you will recognize them.

62. How shall we recognize a Christ follower? What might be a bad fruit in the world to-day?

_____

_____

_____

63. List here the opposites of each of the fruits of the spirit. Example: love/hate

_____

_____

_____

64. If you are a Christian, is it due to the example of another caring Christian? Who was that individual? Write down your experience here.

_____

_____

_____

LET'S TALK A LITTLE ABOUT DISCERMENT AND JUDGMENT

The dictionary describes discernment as follows: to separate or distinguish. Have you ever heard someone say, "Who do you think you are? You're not my judge!" Well, they are right. The definition of the word *judge* is to hear and determine authoritatively, to examine and pass sentence on, to administer justice.

Now let's look at what God's Word has to say. Hebrews 5:14: "But solid food [real and detailed study of God's Word] is for the mature, who by constant use have trained themselves to distinguish good from evil."

As growing Christians we are to learn to distinguish or discern, good from evil. We are to recognize what activity in this world does not please God. However, we are not to judge any man. God himself will judge and pass sentence on each man. Matthew 7:1–2 is quite clear when it says: "Do not judge, or you too will be judged. For in the same way you judge others, you will be judged, and with the measure you use, it will be measured to you."

We could not ask for a clearer message than, "Do not judge."

For the word of God is living and active. Sharper than any double-edged sword, it penetrates even to dividing soul and spirit, joints and marrow; it judges the thoughts and attitudes of the heart. 13 Nothing in all creation is hidden from God's sight. Everything is uncovered and laid bare before the eyes of him to whom we must give an account. (Hebrews 4:12–13)

Since God sees into the heart of every man we must leave the judging of each heart to him.

So What Is Discernment?

We are asked to hold the things of this world up to the light of God's Word. It is in our best interest to question the things of this world, to see if they are good or evil. Then, once we have measured objects and activities by what God's Word tells us, we will learn whether we should embrace or reject them. We go against God's law when we judge our fellow man.

For you were once darkness, but now you are light in the Lord. Live as children of light 9 for the fruit of the light consists in all goodness, righteousness and truth 10 and find out what pleases the Lord. 11 Have nothing to do with the fruitless deeds of darkness, but rather expose them. (Ephesians 5:8–11)

65. Fill in the blanks.
The fruit of the light consists in all
_____,_____and_____.

THE MATURE PLANT BEARS FLOWERS AND FRUIT

As a gardener I love to walk around my garden each morning and find new buds and flowers. This tells me the plants are flourishing. They are in good soil, have plenty of food, light, and water to sustain them. It's great to see little green beads appear on the grape vines, because that means I will have a good crop of grapes later in the season. The grape, which is the fruit of the vine, holds nourishment, flavor, and seed for more plants.

As your plant grows it will form a flower that will be pollinated. When the flower withers, a small bulge can be seen at its base. This is the beginning of the fruit of a plant. It will grow into an apple, if on an apple tree, or a seedpod, if on a poppy plant. Both the edible apple and the inedible poppy seedpod contain seeds for next year's plants. Even herbs, if left uncut, will start flowering and produce seeds.

In the same way God continues to bring men to him. He tells us to share the gospel with others, to plant seeds for the kingdom. In time, those who learn to trust in Christ will do the same. Someday a great harvest of believers will join around his throne to praise him.

A HARVEST OF BLESSINGS

The harvest is all those who have come to the Father. It is God who is glorified; the one who has made us and sacrificed his only son, Jesus, so that we might regain that relationship lost long ago through man's sin in the Garden of Eden.

> John writes about a harvest in John 4:35–37: Do you not say, Four months more and then the harvest? I tell you, open your eyes and look at the fields! They are ripe for harvest. 36 Even now the reaper draws his wages, even now he harvests the crop for eternal life, so that the sower and the reaper may be glad together. 37 Thus the saying, 'One sows and another reaps, is true.'

Following Jesus' ministry, the apostles continued to sow and reap a rich harvest. Men and women who had witnessed their teachings and miracles, done in Jesus' name, believed and became the fruit of that harvest.

> What, after all, is Apollos? And what is Paul? Only servants, through whom you came to believe-as the Lord has assigned to each his task. 6 I planted the seed, Apollos watered it, but God made it grow. 7 So neither he who plants nor he who waters is anything, but only God, who makes things grow. 8 The man who plants and the man who waters have one purpose, and each will be rewarded ac-

cording to his own labor. 9 For we are God's fellow workers; you are God's field, God's building.
(1 Corinthians 3:5–9)

This is what the kingdom of God is like. A man
scatters seed on the ground. 27 Night and day,
whether he sleeps or gets up, the seed sprouts and
grows, though he does not know how. 28 All by
itself the soil produces grain-first the stalk, then
the head, then the full kernel in the head. 29 As
soon as the grain is ripe, he puts the sickle to it,
because the harvest has come. (Mark 4:26–29)

We do not understand all of God's workings, yet
the Spirit makes a change in the heart. From grace,
springs new life. Once our earthly course is finished
God gathers us to himself.

So we come full circle—growing from seeds
planted by others who have gone on before us.
Thank God for the men and women who taught us
about God's salvation, mercy, and grace. We became
new creatures in Christ and are growing to produce
fruit and to plant seeds ourselves. God's plan of salvation goes on and on.

TO EVERTHING THERE IS A SEASON

In the book of Hebrews we read that God gave instruction to his people, the Israelites, through prophets, events, visions, and signs. He asked for offerings

of blood, sacrificed for atonement for sin and for thank offerings. From the Old Testament to the New Testament the season changed and Jesus, God's Son, came to shed his blood as the atoning sacrifice, once and for all. Jesus demonstrated the Father's power and victory over sin and death. In the book of Revelation we are told to expect yet another season; one in which we will be present with the Father for all eternity, where moth does not destroy and pain and suffering are nonexistent.

I have experienced many seasons in my own life. God has called me to seasons of learning, growing, motherhood, loss, sorrow, and joy. I have counseled, and have been counseled. I have had immediate answers to prayer and have had to wait for some answers. God emboldens us for changes in direction and we are to have faith that he has gone before us to prepare the way. Expect God to bring seasons into your life. Each change can be as refreshing and exciting as our earth seasons. Whatever season you may be in right now in your spiritual growth, be assured that your Father in heaven has a reason for it.

The seasons for a gardener are also quite important. For instance, an ear of corn would not tassel or bring a harvest if left in the spring stage. For corn to grow, it has to have many days of summer sun. Pollination must take place from summer insects; nutrients must be provided for growth and development. After the harvest of corn comes a time for the soil to rest or it will yield substandard crops the following year. Often, crops must be rotated to another field entirely to remain healthy and avoid depletion of necessary nutrients in the soil.

God uses the seasons in our lives to replenish, build up, give rest, and mature us. While waiting may be a bit confusing, be assured that you are where you are for a purpose. Here, in these times of change, our faith builds, as a sturdy foundation on which to stand confidently.

Our heavenly father has given us life. He wants us to grow and to know and love him. He wants us to honor him and give him glory. We glorify God by living obedient, fruitful lives, as we ourselves are a demonstration of God's power at work in us through the Holy Spirit.

I hope you never become complacent about God's creation. He set Adam and Eve in a perfect setting and walked with them in the cool of the day because he loved them. God's lessons for life are mirrored even in a simple plant. Remember what you have learned and grow in him.

For complete instruction for feeding and weeding your spiritual life, read God's holy Word, the Bible.

I quote Paul's prayer as my prayer for you as you grow in him.

I pray that out of his glorious riches he may strengthen you with power through his Spirit in your inner being, so that Christ may dwell in your hearts though faith. And I pray that you, being rooted and established in love, may have power, together with all the saints, to grasp how wide and long and high and deep is the love of Christ, and to know this love that surpasses knowledge that you may be filled to the measure of all the fullness of God. Now to him who is able to do immeasurably more than all we ask or imagine, according to his power that is at work within us, to him be glory in the church and in Christ Jesus throughout all generations, for ever and ever. Amen. (Ephesians 3:16–21)

SEED MENTIONED IN THE BIBLE

Actual seeds such as herbs, fruit, tree seeds, coriander, barley, fig, and mustard are mentioned in the Bible. The word *seed* was primarily used in the Old and New Testaments as a synonym for offspring or descendants. For instance, Cain, Adam and Eve's son, was their seed. The word *seed* was also used to represent the message of Christ. An example would be: some planted the seed, others watered it, but God caused it to grow.

BIBLIOGRAPHY

Willard, Dallas. *The Spirit of the Disciplines, Understanding how God changes lives.* HarperCollins, New York, 1988.

Thatcher, Virginia S. *The New Webster Encyclopedic Dictionary of the English Language.* Consolidated Book Publishers, Chicago, 1971.

GLOSSARY

Cold frame

> A cold frame houses your plants as they harden off. It allows you to keep the plants outside even when the evenings get cool. It holds the heat from the sun and keeps the plants warm at night. Using a cold frame eliminates the step of bringing plants in after their allotted time each day outside. It allows them to be left in the cold frame for the entire hardening off period.

Construct cold frame sides, back and front from 5/8-inch plywood. Paint entire box with waterproof stain or outdoor enamel.

Attach a support bar in the middle of the opening to support plastic sheeting.

Attach roll of heavy plastic sheeting to top back of box. This will allow you to cover the plants at night and open the box during daylight in the hardening off phase.

Line the bottom interior of box with landscape fabric. This will keep out plant-eating insects such as slugs. This dark fabric will also capture the heat of the sun and keep your plants warmer when the box is closed at night.

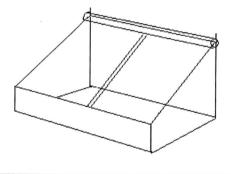

You can also find plans for a cold frame at *www.gardengatemagazine.com* or at your library. For useful information about gardening I like the website *If plants could talk*. Maybe you will want to purchase a book about practical gardening. There are many on the market today.

Cotyledon

The first visual sign of a plant is its double feeder leaves. Some plant varieties will have grass-like thin leaves; others will have a pair of oval leaves. These first, small leaves will wither and die when replaced by the next set of adult plant leaves.

Damping off

This happens when plants are allowed to remain too wet. Fungus begins to form on stems and eventually kills plants.

Grow light

Florescent tube lighting used by gardeners for the purpose of growing plants indoors. Seedlings require bright light immediately after germination. One warm-white 40-watt bulb and one cool-white 40-watt bulb used together are adequate for seed starting and seedling growth. Special grow lights are also suitable, but more expensive.

Below is a diagram showing how to arrange lights and shelves for multiple trays of plants.

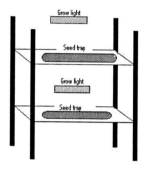

You can find instructions for building a grow light frame from PVC at *http:// www.hort. cornell.edu/gardening/fctsheet/growlite index.html*

Hardening off

When young plants show their adult leaves, they are ready to be introduced to direct sunlight. Over a period of ten to fourteen days and for increasing amounts of time each day, place plants outdoors. Begin the first day by setting plants in shaded area, each day increasing plant's time in the sun. In about ten to fourteen days, plants will be ready for the final move to their permanent site outside.

Photosynthesis

The process by which light energy is utilized to convert carbon dioxide and water into food to be used by plants. Oxygen is released into the air during the process. Light or solar energy is captured by chlorophyll, the green pigment in leaves. It is then converted into chemical energy, which is stored as starch or sugar. These starches and sugars are stored in roots, stems, and fruits. They are available to the plant as food or fuel.

ANSWERS TO QUESTIONS IN THIS STUDY

1. Once you have become a Christian and realize that your sins are forgiven, what should be your reason for doing good things?
   Our reasons for doing good now revolve around our thankfulness for what Christ has done for us. Our deeds are done with a joyfilled heart that is free from the guilt of sin and the fear of death and hell.

2. Requires a personal answer.

3. What are the things Paul prays for?
   He prays for strength for believers through the Holy Spirit's indwelling. He prays for power for believers, so they can understand the depth of God's love. He prays that believers may be filled with all the fullness of God.

4. What is meant by the fullness of God?
   The life that is open to Christ's presence is rooted and grounded in love. This is the widest, longest, highest, and deepest knowledge of all, the very fullness of God. God gives everything its ultimate richness and significance.

5. Who knows God's thoughts?
   The Holy Spirit knows the thoughts of God.

6. How then are we to understand what God wants for us?
   We are to listen with our hearts to what the Holy Spirit tells us.

7. Who does not accept the things that come from the Spirit of God?
   Persons without the Spirit. The individual who has not accepted God, in the person of Jesus Christ.

8. What do Spirit-filled things seem like to the man without the Spirit?
They seem like foolishness to him.

9. Think about the word *established*. How does the dictionary meaning help us understand our establishment by God?
With the help of the dictionary definition we understand that our establishment in God's love means we are securely and permanently fastened to Him.

10. What does renewing of the mind do to transform us?
We no longer think as the world thinks, but are changed to understand the things of God.

11. What length of time does the word *continue* imply in verse six?
Continue, in this verse, means not to stop living in Him. It implies a lifelong commitment of growth and being built up in Him.

12. Look up the word *noble* in the dictionary and write the definition here.
Noble = excellence, worth.

13. What are the characteristics of the person who accepts the Word?

The characteristics are: of noble and good heart, one who hears the word, remembers it, and by persevering produces a good crop.

14. Look closely at the meaning of perseverance. Notice that the dictionary meaning includes the words *long continued application*. What are the implications for the Christian? A Christian, through perseverance, continues to grow and to learn about God for a lifetime.

15. Requires a personal answer.

16. Requires a personal answer.

17. a. How might a person grow by doing a job that takes him out of his comfort zone? A person will grow from this experience through trusting God to supply the power and wisdom for the new challenge.

    b. What are some things one might expect to see God doing during this time? God might teach us a specific lesson. He may use it as a stepping stone to encourage us to even bigger things.

18. Requires a personal answer.

149

19. What does Jesus, the living water, promise those who receive Him?
The water Jesus offers wells up to eternal life.

20. Describe in your own words the characteristics God gave mankind.
Mankind was given rulership over all the earth.

21. How should we apply these characteristics to our lives today?
We should be active in the care and conservation of all God's creation. Using all its resources responsibly because they are gifts from him.

22. What did God place in man's care?
God gave everything earthly to man for his care; birds, beasts, fish, the entire planet.

23. Does this give us a glimpse of the great things God planned for man? Explain.
From the very beginning man was given honor and authority. These were gifts given from a deep love. God wanted a love relationship with man.

24. Who is *us* in verse 26?
Us refers to the three in one: Father, Son and Holy Spirit.

25. Can our deeds/works bring us closer to God?
     No, our good deeds are only love offerings
     to God.

26. Are our practices of discipline penance for
     bad things we've done?
     No, discipline is to train us so that we are
     ready to be godly men and women in all
     circumstances.

27. True or False: The harder I work for God
     the more he will love me.
     False, he loves me with an everlasting, com-
     plete, and perfect love.

28. Should you look for praise from men each
     time you do a good deed?
     No, we should do good deeds for God's
     glory, not our own.

29. On the lines below, list all the things love is
     not.
     Love is not envious, it is not boastful, proud,
     rude, self-seeking, easily angered, a
     rememberer of wrongs, delighted with evil.

30. Now list the things that love is.
     Love is patient, kind, protects, trusts, hopes,
     perseveres, always exists. It is the greatest
     command.

31. We can attain many worthy attributes and still not have love. First Corinthians tell us what these are. List them below.
Speaking in tongues, prophesying, able to fathom mysteries and all knowledge, possess faith, give to the poor, sacrifice one's body to flames.

32. Requires a personal answer.

33. What are some problems that can occur when we exclude water/living water from plants or ourselves?
For plants, exclusion of water can slow, then stop nutrients from traveling throughout the entire plant. Without nutrients and water a plant will quickly wither and die.

For the Christian, the lack of the living water, the exclusion of Jesus in our daily lives, will cause us to experience a lessening of spiritual strength. Our power for living victoriously will diminish.

34. What does it mean to be arrayed in robes of righteousness?
We are changed by salvation through Christ and our sins are covered by his shed blood. We now wear a new robe of righteousness.

35. Requires a personal answer.

36. God has raised us to what position? What do you think this means?
We are raised to be seated with Christ in heaven and a new life as believers in Christ.

37. What will God show us in the coming ages?
He will show us the incomparable riches of his grace, his love and acceptance.

38. What is the gift of God?
Our gift is salvation through faith in Christ Jesus.

39. a. Can we earn our salvation? Explain.
No, we cannot earn our salvation. Our salvation is a gift from God. While we were yet sinners Christ died for us. There is nothing we can do to gain merit or deserve God's love. We must be changed by asking Jesus to come into our heart and life, which makes us perfect through his redeeming blood.

b. How does this make us equal in God's sight?
We are all God's creation and by receiving Jesus, we become equal. No man can boast about how he earned eternal life, because it is an unmerited free gift.

40. Everyone needs money to live. How can money come between us and God?

We can spend so much time making money that we forget about discipline, self-control, and God.

41. How can wealth be used by God?
We can recognize that our wealth has come from him and that we are to use it for his kingdom work. We might give it for a mission project at home or far away. He may ask us to share our wealth to feed the poor or build a church in a remote village in another country.

42. Requires a personal answer.

43. How should we serve God?
He wants us to serve him only, and wholeheartedly.

44. What do these verses tell us that we must eliminate and thin out?
Falsehood, anger, devil's foothold, stealing, unwholesome talk, bitterness, rage, brawling, slander, malice.

45. Requires a personal answer.

46. How is the tongue like a small spark?
Just like a small spark can cause a great fire, the tongue can cause great damage to ourselves and others.

47. How can the tongue be full of deadly poison? Give examples.
    When we use our tongue to spread lies or gossip, it can be deadly to another's reputation. When we deride our children, we damage them emotionally. By using our tongues to hurt others we grieve the Holy Spirit. When we use our tongues for evil practices we diminish our usefulness to God.

48. From this passage list the good things we should strive for.
    Speak truthfully, work and do useful things, share with those in need, let your conversation build others up, let it be a benefit to those who listen. Be kind and compassionate to others, forgiving others as Christ forgave you.

49. Requires a personal answer.

50. Requires a personal answer.

51. What do you think causes people to build their lives (houses) on the sand?
    Perhaps an envious person would choose to spend his life making money to buy more things than those people he envies. He has not learned God's laws, but only how to make and spend money. When life becomes difficult he has no knowledge of God's love

or power. He may die in or from this condition of hopelessness. Remember what many rich tycoons did when the stock market crashed in 1929? They jumped out of windows or shot themselves because they had put all their faith in their fortunes. When their money was gone they thought they had no other reason to live.

52. Describe the differences between the blessed and the wicked.
The blessed delight in the law of the Lord. He thinks about these things continually. He is fruitful and doesn't quit. Whatever he does prospers.

53. How are the wicked like chaff?
They will not withstand God's righteous judgment, nor will they assemble with the righteous. They will perish.

54. Requires a personal answer.

55. What will you do to be able to tell true doctrine from false?
Read God's Word until I have it hidden in my heart. Test all doctrine against God's holy Word.

56. Let's review the three growth stimuli for healthy plants and Christians.

Light - The light of life is found in Jesus Christ.

Light - It helps plants to grow through the process of photosynthesis.

Water - Jesus gives us hope in everlasting life.

Water - It moves nutrients throughout the plant, causing plant growth and health.

Food - God's Word feeds our hearts and minds with necessary and good things.

Food - It gives life-sustaining nutrients to plants and makes them healthier and stronger.

57. Make a list of the comforts the Lord offers his sheep. (Us)

We will not want. He gives us rest and quiet. He restores our souls. He guides us in righteousness. Even in death, we need not fear, for God is with us. He protects us with his rod and staff. He hosts a meal and protects us from the enemy. He soothes with oil and blesses to overflowing. God follows and protects all our days. Finally, we will live with him eternally.

58. Requires personal answer.

59. Requires personal answer.

60. Requires personal answer.

61. Requires personal answer.

62. How shall we recognize Christ's followers? What might be a bad fruit in the world today? We know Christ followers by their fruit. They will produce good things. Today, bad fruit might be impatience. It has become such a problem that we are literally killing each other on the highways. Our impatience causes us to cut off other drivers who make us angry. Driving while angry can make us reckless.

63. List here the opposites of each of the fruits of the spirit.
Love-hate, joy-sadness, peace-restlessness, patience-impatience, kindness-heartlessness, goodness-evil spiritedness, faithfulness disloyalty and faithlessness, gentleness-hardheartedness and cruelty, self-control-no control.

64. Requires personal answer.

65. Fill in the blanks.
The fruit of the light consists in all goodness, righteousness, and truth.

To order additional copies of

FIRMLY
PLANTED
AND
GROWING

Have your credit card ready and call:

1-877-421-READ (7323)

or please visit our web site at
www.pleasantword.com

Also available at:
www.amazon.com
www.barnesandnoble.com

Printed in the United States
23318LVS00001B/4-90